# THE REPUBLIC OF GAMES

# The Republic of Games

*Textual Culture between*
*Old Books and New Media*

ELYSE GRAHAM

McGill-Queen's University Press
Montreal & Kingston • London • Chicago

ISBN 978-0-7735-5338-5 (cloth)
ISBN 978-0-7735-5339-2 (paper)
ISBN 978-0-7735-5420-7 (ePDF)
ISBN 978-0-7735-5421-4 (ePUB)

Legal deposit second quarter 2018
Bibliothèque nationale du Québec

Printed in Canada on acid-free paper that is 100% ancient forest free
(100% post-consumer recycled), processed chlorine free.

Publication has been supported with a grant from the English Fund
for Excellence at Stony Brook University.

We acknowledge the support of the Canada Council for the Arts,
which last year invested $153 million to bring the arts to Canadians
throughout the country.

Nous remercions le Conseil des arts du Canada de son soutien. L'an
dernier, le Conseil a investi 153 millions de dollars pour mettre de l'art
dans la vie des Canadiennes et des Canadiens de tout le pays.

**Library and Archives Canada Cataloguing in Publication**

Graham, Elyse, author
    The republic of games : textual culture between old
books and new media / Elyse Graham.

Includes bibliographical references and index.
Issued in print and electronic formats.
ISBN 978-0-7735-5338-5 (cloth). – ISBN 978-0-7735-5339-2 (paper). –
ISBN 978-0-7735-5420-7 (ePDF). – ISBN 978-0-7735-5421-4 (ePUB)

    1. Electronic publishing. 2. Gamification. 3. Social media. I. Title.

Z286.E43G73 2018          070.5'7973          C2018-900247-6
                                              C2018-900248-4

This book was typeset by True to Type in 11/14 Sabon

# Contents

# Acknowledgments

I want to begin by thanking my parents, Steve and Susan, for their humour and support down the years. I am immensely grateful to my university colleagues for their insight, encouragement, and generosity: Mark Aronoff, Amy Cook, Alix Cooper, Bob Crease, Patricia Dunn, Andrew Flescher, Nicole Galante, Margaret Hanley, Eric Haralson, Clifford Huffman, Heidi Hutner, Justin Johnston, Ann Kaplan, Ken Lindblom, Peter Manning, Celia Marshik, Adrienne Munich, Andrew Newman, Stacey Olster, Douglas Pfeiffer, Rowan Phillips, Elizabeth Rehn, Benedict Robinson, Michael Rubenstein, Jeffrey Santa Ana, Susan Scheckel, Margaret Schedel, August Sheehy, Theresa Spadola, Stephen Spector, Michael Tondre, and Bente Videbaek. In addition, I wish to express special gratitude to my teachers in media studies, book history, and literary studies: Ann Blair, James Buzard, Maria DiBattista, Wai Chee Dimock, Mary Fuller, Diana Henderson, James Paradis, Leah Price, Jeffrey Ravel, and David Thorburn. Robert Darnton taught the first course in book history that I ever took; to him I owe my interest in the field. David Kastan, Catherine Nicholson, and John Williams saw early iterations of this project and offered important advice and encouragement. Conversations with David Bromwich, Nate Matias, William Uricchio, David Weinberger, and Ethan Zuckerman helped me to clarify my thoughts about aspects of this project during the years it was underway. Kathleen Fraser, Kyla Madden, and Kathryn Simpson provided sound editorial guidance. Finally, thanks go to Abigail Droge, Stephanie Holden, Michelle Taylor, and Cooper Wilhelm for being great teachers; to Paul Fry for advice and support; to Erika Supria Honisch for friendship; and to Catherine Curie for listening.

THE REPUBLIC OF GAMES

# Introduction

The question of whether games are art has been almost exhausted in new media studies. The question of whether art is a game is less often asked and more difficult to answer. This book examines the consequences of introducing game mechanics to digital platforms for the production and circulation of text(s). This practice, known in corporate circles as "gamification," has gained widespread popularity online, especially on social-media platforms, fan forums, and other user-generated content platforms. In our platform era, these are no less institutions of publishing than were the newspapers, mass magazines, or *libelles* that defined the literary republics of earlier eras. Indeed, in some cases they reach far larger audiences. Unlike their predecessors, however, these platforms are driven by a unique feature: they are designed to encourage users to generate content as a leisure activity.

Gamification is one of many tools that these platforms utilize to make the production of content feel like play, helping to drive up the free production of content. It often comprises very basic mechanics, such as the ability for users to earn points. A simple example from Facebook: users earn points, so to speak, when others click "like" on a comment, share a comment, or join their "friends" list. But these basic mechanics, which create relative winners and losers among users, combine with other features of these sites to categorically fulfill a minimal definition of a game: voluntary participation on the part of users; a separation from the commercial economy, again on the part of users; consistent rules that govern participation; and a "second-order reality" that separates the environment of the site from the outside world.[1] This book attempts to show that this structural change has wrought larger effects in the textual ecosystem. One consequence is a profound increase in the volume of text produced. Users who write for gamified textual platforms are often extraordinarily prolific – a remarkable fact, given that they write for free. Another consequence is a reliance on user-based systems of information management for dealing with the volume of texts produced. Game structures both produce a problem of textual overload and, in solving this problem, strengthen the hermetic boundaries that separate online textual communities.

I am especially interested in the new cultural and literary formations that have arisen as a result of these mechanics. Humanities scholars still sometimes think in terms of print culture when they set out to delimit the possibilities of new media. They declare that the new machine age holds nothing to fear, for books themselves are machines; that the last great information revolution belonged to the printing press, a narrative in which Zuckerberg typologically refigures Gutenberg; and that the goal of digital scholarship is to build a new Library of Alexandria. Site design, too, often borrows interface metaphors from print culture to help users navigate new technologies: we use *pages* and *bookmarks*, click through *chapters*, interact with *authors*, browse social-media *archives*. But – as we still find it necessary to remind ourselves, and no doubt will for some time – the changes that digital technologies have wrought are not merely mechanical, converting text into hypertext and the page into the webpage, but are importantly and fundamentally social as well. Our republic of letters no longer conforms to a bibliographic framework, although our critical language has not entirely caught up with this.

This book argues that the rise of gamification practices on social-media platforms, which occurred in the wake of Web 2.0 in the first decade of the new millennium, has wrought changes of both scale and scope to our online textual cultures.[2] In previous literary systems, amateur literary production sometimes occurred in contexts of game-play; more often, it occurred in contexts of gift exchange. For example, books of parlour games from early modern Europe include games that reward literary wit. Players would devise poetry as a form of competition rooted in the display of learning, reflecting a time when literature was a class of knowledge that encompassed polite education in general.[3] More recently, literary games like Mad Libs and word jumbles have caught on in the popular culture of print. Yet despite these occasional amusements, for most of literary history, game structures played a negligible role in the production and circulation of literary texts. Textual ecosystems that feature explicit game elements, such that activity in those ecosystems constitutes a game according to a general minimal definition, seem to me to be distinctive of the digital environment, and in particular of the digital environment since Web 2.0. It is a new phenomenon for game structures to subtend the production, circulation, and preservation of texts.

This development raises a number of important questions. Has the rise of gamified platforms for textual production affected the habits, and demographic profiles, of writers? Do traditional literary concepts, such as author, genre, and text, change in the context of game mechanics? What are the effects when "rules of play" add tacit barriers to publication on publishing platforms that otherwise have none? Are gamified textual platforms online sufficiently different from print platforms to constitute a distinctive publishing ecosystem? In this book, I explore these and related issues while drawing on concepts from textual scholarship, game studies, and platform studies.

The platform scholar José van Dijck often refers to the world of social media as an *ecosystem*.[4] The term is meant to signify the interconnectedness of the various social-media platforms that vie for our attention as well as their growing dominance as a general habitat for activity on the web. Thus, for example, Facebook permits users to display on their Facebook pages videos from YouTube, pictures from Instagram, and texts from Twitter, while YouTube, Instagram, and Twitter provide "share" buttons (or the equivalent) that encourage users to display content from those platforms on Facebook.[5] Moreover, countless services and websites that are not themselves social-media platforms rely on social-media platforms as a part of their functioning. For example, the website for *The New York Times*, like most other web instantiations of old-media giants, provides readers with Facebook "share" buttons, as well as other features, such as "trending" lists, that social media has refined.[6] For this reason, van Dijck argues, we can best understand many individual Web platforms by viewing them as parts of a larger "ecosystem of interconnected platforms and applications": "We can only gain insight into the mutual shaping of platforms and apps if we view them as part of a larger online structure where every single tweak affects another part of the system."[7]

Van Dijck further offers reasons for "dissecting specific platforms" as a method of inquiry into larger phenomena shared across the social-media ecosystem. Notably, this is an ecosystem in which a few platforms hold extraordinary dominance. Facebook, in particular, exerts profound influence over the development of applications, communities, and even norms of interactivity in other areas of the web, making the site, at present, a necessary item to consider in any study of social media at large. "Facebook is the largest social network site in the United States and in Europe, with the highest penetration among Internet users." As of June 2016, the site boasted an estimated 1.68 billion users.[8] Certain features of Facebook have become pervasive across the Web. Countless websites have incorporated Facebook's "like" button into their functionality, enabling users to award content from these sites "likes" on Facebook: "Three months after its introduction, more than 350,000 external websites had already installed the feature."[9] Still other websites use similar features that enable users to award points to content. In keeping with her focus on sociality writ large, van Dijck discusses the "like" button and similar features in terms of connectivity, or their ability to link persons, entities, and ideas. In this book, I consider another aspect of these features: their tacit inclusion of scoring mechanisms, and thereby of terms of competition. Through a variety of mechanisms, which include formal scoring mechanisms such as "likes," "kudos," "favourites," comments, and followers; rewards for superior outcomes that are either contained to the microsystem of the site or the ecosystem of social media, such as "trending" or "viral" status via ranking algorithms;

protocols built into site operations that establish tacit terms of play; and higher-order systems of play that users build atop, and sometimes in opposition to, embedded protocols – through such diverse yet affiliated mechanisms, the larger communicative systems that social media pervades incorporate variously basic or complex suites of game mechanics.[10] We cannot fully understand social and textual phenomena online without taking these mechanics into account.

In the terminology of the ecosystem, I use two particular sites, Facebook and Archive of Our Own, in a function comparable to that of an ecologist's *quadrat*, a tool that researchers use to delineate and study a representative part of an ecosystem.[11] As I show, distinctive features of these platforms can provide new insights into broader patterns of textual production and circulation online. Indeed, as I discuss in chapter 4, the triumph of social media may have added another structure – game – to the traditional new-media "dyad" of narrative and database.[12] Or at least the Web has made more visible, more widely discussed, and more complex, the consumption of traditional media through game-like structures. Fans of the book series *A Song of Ice and Fire*, for example, can use gamified social-media platforms to exchange theories, engage in question-and-answer sessions about "headcanons" ("writing memes"), write new stories based on the exchange of prompts and fills, devise drinking games, and play fan-made roleplaying games. This is in addition to the gamified environments for fiction-making that (as chapter 3 discusses) constitute fan fiction sites. These examples illustrate the ways in which even traditional media forms are being reconstituted as games in the digital environment.

With this in mind, this book attends, in part, to the claim that game mechanics bear on a wider online culture that emphasizes voluntary, free activity. Following the work of Richard Barbrook, scholars of new media have often appealed to the gift as a framework for understanding the prevalence of free exchange online. In the decades since Barbrook first gave a name to "hi-tech gift culture," the mystique surrounding the free production of content online has only grown. In recent years, such leading social critics as Lawrence Lessig and Yochai Benkler have investigated the prevalence of digital production in voluntary and non-commercial forms. These authors share the general optimism of the Berkman-Klein set toward amateur creativity online; in their policy discussions, this often translates into a corresponding concern over how amateur creativity can survive on a monetized Web. Steven Hetcher, for example, working on the assumption that agents in the online economy of sharing act out of concern for others, suggests that sites that host amateur content risk falling prey to "the problem of maintaining altruistic motivations to participate as the project [becomes] larger and more impersonal."[13] In a different domain, Karen Hellekson, a scholar of fan culture, describes online fan production as a form of Maussian gifting, basing her identification of fan production with gifting mainly on the presence of free exchange: "Exchange in the fan community is made up of three elements related to the gift: to give, to receive, to reciprocate."[14] And in the popular marketplace, digital dystopians have denounced the rise of user-generated content as a combination of gift and theft. In his 2007 book *The Cult of the Amateur*, Andrew Keen criticizes amateur cultures online for recycling and sharing intellectual property to which they have no claim.[15]

These discussions have not yet taken into account the rise of game play as a model for designing textual spaces online. Many scholars have taken interest, however, in expanding our taxonomy of free online labour, a project to which this book seeks to contribute. The legal scholar Steven Hetcher, for example, argues that ideas about altruistic amateurs "do not apply to the sorts of amateur content found on dominant commercial sites like Facebook and YouTube," where "users upload content because it serves their purposes – they do not understand themselves to be engaged in altruistic activities."[16] Until we take such major platforms into account, our understanding of online structures of textual production and circulation will be incomplete. Gamification offers a way of understanding one province of voluntary production in the digital environment without appealing to gift-giving or altruism as motivations. It can also help us to situate the new amateur publishing cultures flourishing online in the long history of amateur publishing.

■

The chapters that follow are a focused collection of essays on the effects of gamification on textual ecosystems online: how a game economy differs from a gift economy; how the design of specific web platforms shapes activity on those platforms in the form of game play; what effects game structures have had on textual ecosystems; and how terminology from print culture that is still in use online both fits the game model and obscures real user activity. They follow a general thematic progression, focusing in turn on the creators of social-media platforms, who are in a privileged position to register, and respond to, changes in the material conditions of textuality; writing communities, who build higher-order systems from the mechanics they're given; and scholars, who must reconcile their efforts to gain critical distance from the new system with their own structural subordination within it. Together, the chapters undertake to show that embedding game structures into the operations of digital platforms – even when doing so entails adding only small mechanics, such as points and badges – can have larger cumulative effects on patterns of textual production and circulation. As more creative labour and literary work is digitally born, this phenomenon is important to recognize and understand. As a space of play, a space of competition, a space of flow, the game as a formal arena enables platforms to keep the reader perpetually engaged in the activities of reading, navigating, and adding to the body of the text. Fan communities, in their exuberant productivity, help to illuminate this dynamic but do not exhaust it; the lay citizens of network culture likewise mix time, effort, and resources to create content that they give away for free, in part because the spaces they inhabit are configured as worlds of play not labour. The magic circle both protects the space of play from the burdens of the outside world and unifies the rewards of the game with the pleasures of the act of play. An account of networked textuality that focuses on game elements can help us to better situate textual cultures online in a larger historical matrix. A complicated root system of genealogies ties networked communication to the histories of film, theatre, book history, communications, and literature; to these we can add the history of games.

The first chapter, "Play and the Platform Era," considers the conditions surrounding the gamification of social-media platforms. Traditionally, critics have explained the circulation of content online in terms of a gift economy of production and exchange. As I show, however, the social basis of content production online can be better understood in terms of a game economy – a point that Silicon Valley understands perfectly well, and for which it has coined the limited but useful term "gamification." Indeed, I argue, game structures have come to provide the dominant mode of literary production online, both in the broad sense of literature as written texts and in the specific sense of literature as written works of the imagination. If we wish to better understand the character, for example, of born-digital archives for the production of fiction; if we wish to better understand online spaces in which audiences gather to consume fiction produced in other media formats; then we need to look carefully at the communities, values, and practices that the digital environment fosters that the print environment did not. Such an approach can help us to embrace the best of prior textual scholarship while reaching out to different media genealogies.

The second chapter, "The Republic of Games," examines digital textual production within the frameworks of game studies. Focusing on Facebook, I show how social-media platforms utilize game mechanics to engage users. Outlining traits of social-media platforms like feedback, point mechanisms, voluntary activity, and a bounded environment, I explore the relationship between the gamification practices that thrive online and the importance of reader presence in design considerations for the webpage.

The third chapter, "The Great Game," argues that media scholars can better understand the forms of amateur fiction that are thriving in the digital environment by making use of terms and perspectives from game studies. Many of the most popular platforms on the Internet today, including social news platforms and social-media platforms, are organized in the form of games; I argue that online fiction archives, too, have a genealogy rooted in games rather than one rooted in anthologies, poetry collections, libraries, and other strictly literary formats. This argument has implications for efforts to theorize the production of fiction on the Internet, and indeed to theorize the reception of fiction in other media forms in the Internet age.

The fourth chapter, "The Printing Press as Metaphor," examines our popular uses of historical metaphor to explain a period of dramatic change in our media environment. It is as common today for us to use the printing press as the central unit of measure in estimations of information history as it is for us to discuss our current circumstances in terms of an "information revolution." Surrounded as we are by these analogies, it seems fair to ask what purposes they serve. As I show, this rhetoric offers a powerful reminder of the extent to which technological discourse, inside as well as outside the academy, is obliged to respond to market imperatives. Indeed, this set of tropes participates in a longer history of technological rhetoric that utilizes slippery language to shape the story of technological change in a form with popular appeal, a rhetoric that includes our uses of the word "technology" itself. It also suggests that the much-discussed tension between the operations of the digital environment, on the one hand, and narratives and metaphors belonging to print culture, on the other, is usefully complicated by attention to game mechanics. The linguistic and visual cues of the page, the bookmark, the archive, so forth, which, as many scholars have discussed, serve as handles to help users interact with digital platforms, represent a useful and knowing anachronism insofar as their histories provide concepts that we use as tools to navigate digital environments. Still, we must take every opportunity to document the changes in literary and social relations that are emerging in the spaces around these anachronisms.

The factors that define the "digital revolution" are not merely technological; they are cultural, social, and methodological. On digital social networks, users follow patterns of writing, interacting, and meaning-making that differ from the habits of older media communities. In online literary communities, users build systems of higher-level, rule-bound play that exceed the requirements of their media architectures and depart from the conventions of literary tradition. In the "real life" spaces where new-media technology is created, game play skills and online forums, hoodies and sneakers, help to establish the boundaries of a distinctive culture whose values enter the shape of new technologies. The aim of this book is to detail one aspect of these social changes: the gamified structures of production and circulation that now dominate the textual culture of social media. In both trade publishing and the avant-garde, print culture lacked the constellation of properties, such as winning conditions, that constitute the minimal definition of a game; print culture also lacked specific forms of creativity, collectivity, and sociability that are becoming increasingly familiar features of the ecosystem of connective media. The chapters that follow represent an expansion and application of these ideas.

# 1

# Play and the Platform Era

This chapter presents an overview of the conditions surrounding the gamification of social-media platforms. The triumph of social-media platforms during the first decade of the twenty-first century, as platform-based social media and prosumer applications became major forces in online publishing, exacerbated an existing textual condition that linked the viability of a webpage with constant user activity. Digital textuality has become more subject to a condition of liveness and fluidity than even prophets of the fluid text, such as Jerome McGann and Bernard Cerquiglini, once proposed. Game mechanics have become an important, though often overlooked, means of fostering this activity. Feedback systems, scoring mechanisms, voluntary participation, and higher-level cultures of emergent play inform user-generated content production on social-media platforms such as Facebook, YouTube, and Twitter. Terms and models from the study of games can help us to better understand not only the culture of connective media, but also the forces that sustain the new labour regime that Alexander Galloway has described as "ludic capitalism."[1] Building on the work of Richard Barbrook in the 1990s, critics have often discussed free labour on the Internet in terms of a gift economy of production and exchange. As I show, however, the social conditions of a great deal of textual production and exchange in the digital environment can be better understood in terms of a game economy that derives, in large part, from a suite of commonplace practices in user interface design that Silicon Valley refers to as gamification.

*The Republic of Games* argues that we must bring gamification and its effects into our view of textual studies if we are to participate in, design for, and theorize emerging forms of literary practice in the digital environment.

■

As Jerome McGann argues, understanding the "textual condition" of a literary system requires attention to the social and material conditions of production and transmission.[2] His work represents an era of new directions in textual scholarship – one in which scholars moved toward giving as much attention to the activities of agents around texts as they did to the formal features of texts themselves – that remains salutary as we encounter the formal excitements of the Web. If the movement of textual production online only entailed superficial changes to the formal properties of the text – adding formal excitements like hyperlinking; removing physical properties like weight and scent – that would be one thing. But the social dynamics that govern media ecosystems online differ, sometimes dramatically, from those of earlier media ecosystems. The Web has wrought important changes in the practices, communities, and narratives by which we construe ourselves as consumers and producers of texts. In many cases, the social conditions of the production and reception of texts online differ so thoroughly from their former existence as to change the text's field of activity altogether. At some time in the past twenty years, digital texts stopped being texts in the specific sense that has held for centuries – a sense that Alvin Kernan has theorized in terms of a bibliographic culture whose values were externalized in the institutional structures of publishers, bookstores, libraries, and archives.[3]

These changes are complicated by the fact that we still use design features and terminology from print culture when we navigate textual environments online. The most obvious form this reminiscence takes is the digital "page," which has been the subject of abundant critical discussion.[4] This kind of skeuomorphism can tempt us to seek out the spirit of print culture online, either because we wish to emphasize that new dynamics tap into eternal constants of human culture (mythmaking, storytelling) or because we hope that digital media will enable us to realize the best hopes of the bibliographic past: to create, in short, a new Library of Alexandria. Thus, for example, new cultures of voluntary textual circulation can seem to recapitulate the old: long before the Web, there existed communities of writers who circulated texts freely, observing a gift economy of literary production that superficially resembles the "gift economy" that Richard Barbrook identifies on-line. But many of the structures of textual production and exchange that govern social-media platforms never applied in either trade publishing or the literary avant-garde. I am interested in accounts that mark these different terms of production, many of them systematized as policy and mandated as code; understood this way, the "textual condition" of many parts of the Web emphasizes the space and terms of play over the work produced.

This book argues that a digital work is best understood not as a text, but as a living entity, an ecosystem.[5] One sign of this condition is the degree to which textual cultures in the digital environment emphasize change, new activity, and interaction among users. Not the least of the many reasons that people spend time on websites is in order to hear "ambient noise": the chatter of other living souls. A class that the University of Pennsylvania recently offered to its students, titled "Wasting Time on the Internet," described economies of attention in the digital environment as relying, in important ways, on "aimless drifting and intuitive surfing."[6] Indeed, "surfing" and "browsing," the functional terms we use to describe user activity on the Web, are specific descriptions of capricious, untidy behaviour, favouring exploration over retrieval and open to trivial and serious information alike.[7] When we surf the Web, we don't want to see something *timeless*; we want to see something *new*. Notably, if a website stops being updated, we refer to it as "dead," an expression that would sound absurd if we used it to refer to a book. The vital energy of websites consists, for us, in visible change. One scholar has even proposed that we regard the network era as a new age of urbanization, since a defining trait of the urban environment, that people live close together in chattering, anonymous crowds, can define our social experience even in rural areas, so long as the blogosphere is only a click away.[8]

Certainly, the companies that build and run websites understand their business to consist, in large part, of building and curating audiences. They design user interfaces to keep users wandering the premises; they encourage users to interact, not merely with the site's features, but with each other; and they incorporate into the site's functionality elements – like feedback and competition – that engage users and turn reading into interactive play. The arena that generates new material is more important, in social and economic terms, than the material generated.

An understanding of a digital text as an entity that is always in motion, always in progress, never the property of any one person, challenges venerable ideas about creativity and authorship. As a starting point, a digital text is not fixed – not even within the kind of usable fiction that Bernard Cerquiglini, for example, describes.[9] The text's location with respect to other texts on the "page," which helps to create paratextual meaning, is also not fixed, since new contributions from users, as well as algorithms that reorganize the page, can keep this ordering susceptible to change in perpetuity. Often, the writer can edit or delete the text at any time; thus we cannot cite the text – for example, by creating a hypertext link – with certainty that the text a future reader retrieves will be identical with the one we read. In time, the hyperlink might not lead to a text at all. The phenomenon of "link rot," in which hyperlinks lead to web pages that no longer exist, is already a major problem for writers and readers online.[10] Moreover, to a degree that did not appear even in newspapers, the texts that define the character of many digital platforms are corporate productions. A passage of text that appears on a social-media site may return only thin meaning to traditional hermeneutics. If we want to understand the "textual condition" online, we might fare better if we looked, as with a game of soccer, at the wider interaction between the rules of play, the behaviour of the players, and, in the case of a single agent, the forms of identity, performance, and expression that a specifically virtual and co-performative arena mandates.[11]

Cerquiglini, along with McGann and D.F. McKenzie, led, in the late twentieth century, what Michael Groden calls a "sea change" in the field of textual scholarship, a challenge to the very idea that scholars should seek to recover a fixed authentic text.[12] Rather, they argued, literary texts can only exist as historically specific artifacts, and therefore literary works are hybrid, mutable, and mobile. The rise of digital technologies undoubtedly influenced this critical transition; if the dream of a reliable literary text haunted philological practice throughout the twentieth century, now scholars came to regard the very concept of a definitive text as a product of the logos of print technology. In practical terms, digital media provided the new textual scholarship with ideal tools for critical editing: versioned editions, which enable users to "display and compare multiple versions of texts," could demonstrate the fluidity of texts across their history of publication.[13] Kathleen Fitzpatrick and Susan Schreibman, among others, have further shown the possibilities for open, flexible editing that digital media extend.[14]

McGann situates his most recent study of the digital turn in the library, portraying the library, in an era of hacker-culture "labs," as a prototype and archetype, the great lab of humanistic creation: "The library, research as well as local-public, is the storm centre of these changes because the library is the home base of general education for the citizen as well as the research and teaching humanist, as the laboratory is the home base of the physical scientist."[15] In this, he draws on a venerable trope in the tradition of defences of the humanities: the library as a symbol, an emblem, of knowledge as a bibliographic chain of being. Alvin Kernan, a great if premature elegist of the "republic of letters," sounded an even more elaborate variation on this theme in the 1980s, when the major threat to philology could seem to be deconstructive criticism, which at least used the old weaponry of printed books and journals:

Actual and imaginary libraries ... are important parts of our culture, one of the few points at which we can actually examine society's conception of knowledge and its organization. There are other places as well at which the "knowledge tree" becomes visible – encyclopedias, some philosophies (Aristotle, for example, or Kant), academies of arts and sciences, school curricula and university departmental structures – but the library is particularly revealing because it contains the primary sources of information – printed books – dictates the methods by which they can be approached and studied, and schematizes their principal modes of organization in the shelving departments and the catalogue. The library focuses the intellectual world and provides a paradigm of consciousness, what a society knows and how it knows it.[16]

The challenge of hooking up this "knowledge tree" to the networked environment has been the subject of many important studies that inquire into the relationship between new media and the traditional codes and structures of bibliography. Along with McGann, N. Katherine Hayles, Kathleen Fitzpatrick, and Johanna Drucker have been prominent theorists of digital textuality. Their work demonstrates the complexity that attends the adaptation of textual practices to the digital environment.[17] At the same time, the new field of platform studies, exemplified by scholars such as José van Dijck and Christian Fuchs, has shown the importance of using codes from old media as operational aids in new media.[18] Not accidentally, but rather as a matter of design, do we find a highly visible lineage tracing back from digital machines to "textual machines." Yet even as they take into account the differences between old and new media, these discussions register conflicting rhetorical interests, a situation that chapter 4 will discuss in terms of Bourdieu's "dominated dominants": we respond to the necessity, in an era that can seem at risk of throwing out the books with the card catalogue, to make significance claims on behalf of print; and yet those same significance claims come close, at times, to imagining the future as a wired form of prior bibliographic institutions.[19]

McGann relies for some of his scene-setting on a series of comparisons between "the Internet" and great libraries past and present, such as the Library of Alexandria and the Bodleian Library. These precedents, he says, "can help us navigate through our emerging internetwork. We gain a better perspective on the limits and capacities of our digital rooms because others have worked in the same rooms in different times and circumstances and with different interests and purposes."[20] This book builds upon his lead and extends some of the same critical practices: the study of the social relations and material bases that inform the production and circulation of texts. But it examines a different object: the unstable, born-digital ecosystem of social-media textual platforms. The people in the "room" that these platforms represent have a significantly different social architecture from the people in the "room" of the library.[21] McGann's concerns in his 2014 book sometimes prompt him to bypass social dynamics in favour of the similarities between bit-based and atom-based information systems. For example, code appears in both software and libraries: "The encoding system for the Library of Alexandria was the Greek alphabet."[22] My concerns prompt me to look for the gaps in the analogy between the spaces of bibliography and the digital spaces of textual production and circulation. As the creators of Web-based platforms are discovering, despite their reliance on the paper archive as an interface metaphor to aid user navigation, the "room" of these platforms is not the same as the rooms of the Bodleian, the Beinecke, and the British Museum. A digital space that organized itself using the ontologies and social infrastructures of the Library of Alexandria would not need torches; it would ensure its own destruction, this time by abandonment. The new room shares some of the features of the old rooms, but here gravity works differently and the walls have shifting orientations. Perhaps most importantly, if the new room is empty for long enough, it ceases to exist.

The environment of the Web, which the hypertext theorist Robert Coover called a "noisy, restless, opportunistic, superficial, e-commerce driven, chaotic realm, dominated by hacks, pitchmen and pretenders, in which the quiet voice of literature cannot easily be heard," is profoundly shaped by the need for living traffic. It *makes* it. Because of this, more than anything else, its social and material conditions differ from those of the great age of print.[23] Like all editorial institutions, the entities that run the platforms I discuss engage in what McGann calls "literary pragmatics," translating ideas about textuality into tools for using texts and making them useable; these ideas draw upon the history of literature, but, to an extent unprecedented in literary history, they also draw upon media logics that developed apart from literature.[24] The resulting changes in our textual culture, though they can seem small individually, are producing startling results: one that I will emphasize is incredible productivity on the part of writers. For now, we may easily be able to distinguish between professional writers with reputable publishers, earning fees or royalties, and perhaps earning a place in public life and a literary canon, and "amateur" writers who blog and contribute to social-media platforms; in other words, we may feel able to distinguish between writing that is worth reading, critically reflecting on, and remembering, and writing that is pedestrian, functional, and transitory. But this dichotomy is rapidly breaking down, which makes it incumbent upon scholars thinking about the future of literary creativity to develop new hermeneutics.

■

In this book, I draw many of my examples from fan culture, as it provides a particularly potent illustration of the distinctive relationship between consumption and production that thrives on the Web. One of the first books to discuss extensively the productive basis of fan culture was Henry Jenkins's *Textual Poachers*, which argues that fans actively appropriate media texts for their own unauthorized uses.[25] In the decades since Jenkins's book first appeared, technological changes – in the processing power of personal computers, the cost of digital authoring tools, and the ease of publishing on the Web – have led to an explosion in the kinds of activity he describes. Fan creations now pervade the Web on blogs, message boards, and dedicated social-media platforms, where users produce – gratis – discussion, critical glosses, artwork, stories, songs, videos, podcasts, wallpapers, screen shots, and more.[26] As recently as 2013, Anne Jamison was able to ground a book on the plausible assertion that "fanfiction is taking over the world."[27]

In some media industries, this kind of fan production has become an important part of the business. Consider, for example, the computer game industry, which has come to rely on an activity called "modding" – a term for the modification of computer games by unpaid fans, who manipulate the source code of games to add new players, levels, and even worlds of play.[28] Because "mods," which require the original software in order to run, can extend a game's shelf life by years or decades, game producers have come to treat them almost as unofficial licences and sequels.[29] Categorically, modding is labour: modders devote long hours to programming; they create new products, expand the audience of existing products (for instance, by adding players from Latin American baseball leagues to games based on Major League baseball), and build thriving online communities that support official franchises.[30] The benefits they confer on the game industry are tremendous, and these benefits only happen because modders see their labour as play. "The precarious status of modding as a form of unpaid labour is veiled by the perception of modding as a leisure activity, or simply as an extension of play."[31]

The formal ambiguity of this leisure activity, which has contributed to the challenges that commentators have found in discussing it, has helped to maintain its hold on fans. The difficulty of classifying modding as an activity is what makes it such a fecund source of free labour for the game industry. "Modding and other, similar forms of 'free labour' do not fit the categories of wage labour, freelance or voluntary work, and neither do they fit the categories of leisure, play or art."[32] Ultimately, the belated categorization of modding as play, at least from the perspective of those who engage in it, enables the game industry to exploit the free labour of modders. Some media scholars think this fact impels us to change the system. For example, Abigail De Kosnik has argued that official media producers should compensate the labour of fans. For De Kosnik, the ultimate value of viewing fan labour as "real" labour lies in recovering the worth and dignity of a specifically feminine category of unpaid and undervalued labour – rather like, one might suggest as an analogy, the unpaid labour of housewives according to the critiques of first-wave feminism: "Fans' profuse contributions to the Internet can be regarded … as labor. Online fan productions constitute unauthorized marketing for a wide variety of commodities – almost every kind of product has attracted a fandom of some kind ... Fan activity, instead of being dismissed as insignificant and a waste of time at best and pathological at worst, should be valued as a new form of publicity and advertising, authored by volunteers, that corporations badly need in an era of market fragmentation. In other words, fan production is a category of work."[33]

I argue that this analogy draws on incomplete social frameworks, and that a new kind of attention to the design of the digital platforms on which these activities take place, as well as the social configurations of the users who understand themselves to be at play, can help us to better understand this behaviour. In chapter 3, I examine areas of fan culture online that, unlike modding, revolve around the production of texts, but, like modding, entail free and voluntary content production. Although I am not as confident as De Kosnik that twenty-first-century culture looks down on fan activity, I agree that fan labour can illuminate important features of the relationship between work and leisure in the network era.[34] Literary systems have always maintained close, if complicated, relationships with systems of economic production: for the patronage system, writing communities based on gift exchange; for the different conditions of capitalist society, a commercial publishing system that took advantage of print technology.

Although my focus is primarily on writers and texts, the ambiguities that I investigate reflect a more general ambiguity, based on social and technological change, of our historical moment: for the idea that work and leisure are still the distinct entities they were in the nineteenth and twentieth centuries has led to the misclassification of activities on which we spend large portions of our time. Fan culture, which has thrived online, has often puzzled onlookers who have tried to define fandom's relationship with commerce, with critics unable to decide whether fandom belongs to God or Mammon. Like many proponents throughout history of expanded authorial rights, De Kosnik adheres to the Lockean idea that we create intellectual property when we mix our labour with raw materials. Following the lead of Jenkins, who has argued forcefully for a view of fans as active rather than passive readers, she emphasizes that fans actively rework the cultural materials they consume: "It is not the fan who is devoted to the object so much as the object that serves the needs of the fan – and, initially, it does not do a very good job of that; the fan must invest work into the object to customize the object to better suit the fan's wishes."[35]

For De Kosnik, the reason for the economic imbalance between fans and "official producers" lies in a mistaken self-denial on the part of fans: "many fans ... think of their motives as purer than those of official producers and see themselves as above questions of market value, advertising, and sales."[36] Similarly, the media scholar Matt Hills identifies an ideological contradiction at the heart of fandom, since fan activity appears to be simultaneously consumerist (fans build their cities on commercial franchises) and anti-consumerist (fans produce goods that they give away for free): "While simultaneously 'resisting' norms of capitalist society and its rapid turnover of novel commodities, fans are also implicated in these very economic and cultural processes. Fans are, in one sense, 'ideal consumers' since their consumption habits can be very highly predicted by the culture industry, and are likely to remain stable. But fans also express anti-commercial beliefs (or 'ideologies,' we might say, since these beliefs are not entirely in alignment with the cultural situation in which fans find themselves)."[37]

Hills's resolution to this problem is to describe fan culture as split into conflicting forces: one side, which he terms "anti-commercial ideology," rejects the notion that fans participate in commercial activities as being *infra dig*; the other, which he terms "commodity-completist," embraces the commodity fetishism at the centre of fan activity, which strengthens media works as commodities by giving them a longer shelf life and a larger base of potential consumers.[38] This allows him to define the terms of an apparent contradiction by which fans add value to commodities through their labour while refusing to acknowledge that their value-adding activities constitute labour. The delicacy of this argument leaves us poised on a paradox, however, and may suggest that something is wrong with the assumptions that gird it. In this book I argue that descriptions of cultures of free exchange online in terms of a "gift economy" risk making an unnecessary paradox of online behaviour at large.

The most direct source of the gift-culture model of online activity is the social theorist Richard Barbrook, who introduced his concept of the "hi-tech gift economy" in an influential 1998 article. He published an updated version in 2005.[39] In it he argues that, while early theorists of the Web predicted that network culture would result in "one – and only one – method of organizing labor: the commodity or the gift," ultimately the Web resolved into a separated mixture: "money-commodity and gift relations are not just in conflict with each other, but also co-exist in symbiosis." The separate partners in this symbiosis are a "public element," namely the state-funded researchers who built Arpanet and engineered the Web's early physical architecture; a "corporate element," namely Silicon Valley; and, finally, a "gift economy," which represents most user activity online. However, this remains an uneasy symbiosis at best, with the partners locked in eternal conflict. The gift economy of blogging, pirating, and peer-to-peer sharing aims to subvert Silicon Valley's market economy in favour of "anarcho-communism," while the market economy aims, by transforming technologies into commodities and user activity into advertising data, to put the digital commons into private hands.[40]

As Barbrook notes, early theorizing about free exchange on the Web often took its cue from Marcel Mauss's classic work, *The Gift*, which identifies gift exchange as a key aspect of our tribal past.[41] Mauss focuses his discussion on Polynesian tribes that practised the potlatch, a gift-giving ritual that bound the givers with ties of kinship, hospitality, and obligation. In referencing Mauss, media theorists conjured for the network era a utopian future, warm and personal despite its metallic sheen; because gift exchange, unlike the dead hand of commodity exchange, implies solidarity and kinship, its return would help to restore the lost intimacy of older ways of life.[42] Not coincidentally, this utopian vision harmonizes with the media theory of Walter Ong and Marshall McLuhan, who argued that electronic technology will return us to the holistic communication of tribal society.[43]

However, the Maussian model of gift exchange fits the online environment only imperfectly. It is true that the architecture of the World Wide Web facilitates free exchange; on peer-to-peer networks, the cost of making and sharing copies of documents is zero.[44] And it is true that social conventions online make a virtue of free exchange. Barbrook describes technological and social architectures of free exchange in terms of widening ripples of virtue: scholars, who publish their work freely in exchange for professional credit, adhere to a gift economy by default; the open-source communities that built Linux, Apache, and Firefox adhere to a gift economy by principle; and the bloggers and tweeters who grew up with desktop publishing adhere to a gift economy by tradition, following the practices they have always known. "From scientists through hobbyists to the general public, the charmed circle of users was slowly built up through the adhesion of many localized networks to an agreed set of protocols." As a result, "cyber-communism" has quietly carved out a parallel economy within our capitalist formation: "When they go on-line, almost everyone spends most of their time participating within the gift economy rather than engaging in market competition." Ultimately, Barbrook argues, this shift is an inevitable consequence of technological advances that, by increasing leisure time and disposable income in industrialized nations, frees up their members for the gift economy: "By working for money during some of the week, people can now enjoy the delights of giving gifts at other times."[45]

Still, the fact that capital retains a powerful hold on this ostensible gift society leaves Barbrook's idea of a gift economy as a circle in need of squaring. Barbrook tries to naturalize the tension between these ideas by describing this as a case of unlikely symbiosis: the digital economy is locked in an inescapable conflict between what is free ("the gift economy") and what is commodified ("the money economy"), with each forever attempting to undermine the other: "The potlatch and the commodity remain irreconcilable."[46] Digital capitalists have not only enclosed and privatized social spaces of voluntary labour, as Barbrook feared they would; they have designed those spaces with an eye to maximizing user activity. A traditional potlatch takes place only periodically; the games of tweeting, blogging, liking, and sharing never cease.

■

If the Web started out as a gift economy, its transition into a game economy is a natural outgrowth of a larger dynamic. As the media scholar Tiziana Terranova argues, the Web consists primarily of voluntary labour, and has done so since its inception.[47] Debates over the nature and meaning of this labour have crowded the history of new media; one of the first attention-grabbing disputes over free labour on the Web occurred in 1999, when seven of America Online's chat room "volunteers," an army of more than 10,000 AOL users "whose duties included monitoring electronic bulletin boards, hosting chat-rooms, enforcing the Terms of Service agreement (TOS), and even creating content," filed a complaint with the U.S. Department of Labor, arguing that they should receive back wages for their work.[48] The reason that AOL felt the need to recruit so many volunteers is that online spaces tend to require continuous updating simply to stay in place: website owners must update user interfaces in order to keep them relevant; content contributors must update photos, tweets, and blog entries in order to pull in traffic; and programmers must update software to keep it operational and secure.[49] Terranova argues that the "immaterial" forms of production that characterize the postmodern economy can be more labour-intensive than their material predecessors – a circumstance of which the Web, which as an economic necessity makes a vast industry of free labour, is the most potent expression. "Simultaneously given and unwaged, enjoyed and exploited, free labor on the Net includes the activity of building Web sites, modifying software packages, reading and participating in mailing lists, and building virtual spaces on MUDs and MOOs."[50]

The Web encompasses many ecosystems of unpaid and barely paid labour, which put the industrial separation of work and leisure – or at least their separate valuations – to serious tests.[51] The sociologist Andrew Ross has catalogued some examples. One is "content farms": websites that host low-quality, hastily produced articles and videos designed to trigger search queries and to show up on the first page of Google search results. Content farms generate story ideas by means of algorithms that take into account popular search terms, the ranking of specific terms in search engine results, keywords that are garnering high prices from advertisers, and existing stories on various topics; based on the results, the farms assign stories to their contributors – thousands of freelance writers and videographers – who receive a low fee for each piece. As of 2009, Demand Media, one of the largest content farms, was producing 4,000 articles and videos per day.[52] News and gossip sites like the *Huffington Post*, although they often produce higher-quality content, operate by similar means, relying on contributors to produce content for free or low pay. The distance between these kinds of sites and content farms is not fixed. As Ross notes, "The AOL Way," a strategic plan for AOL that found its way online in 2011, "revealed how it would pay a pittance to in-house writers who were expected to write up to 10 blog articles per day, each prepped for search engine friendliness and for ad exposure."[53]

Crowdsourcing is perhaps the most visible form of the free-labour ethos online. It is also the most celebrated, combining as it does the barn-raising romance of participatory culture with the optimism of techno-libertarianism; it is no surprise that the term first appeared in *Wired* magazine, the voice of business-friendly pop futurism.[54] The print marketplace has found a thriving industry in books that discuss how to exploit the activity of "the hive mind." These books tend to attribute the success of participatory media to universal psychological factors, such as our natural altruism and gregariousness, combined with the social factor of a rise in spare time.[55] However, acquiring a crowd is more difficult than these books sometimes suggest. The networked environment is littered with "crowdsourced" projects that, bereft of contributors, died in the bud.

A category that Ross does not include in his taxonomy, but that is implicit, I think, in his discussion, is the focus of this book: communities of content production and circulation on social media and fan sites. As I discussed above, commentators sometimes treat the free labour of these communities as a problem of exploitation:

the "communal ethos of fandom" is too pure, too disdainful of commercial interests, to acknowledge their role in a profit-making enterprise.[56] In chapter 3, I examine these communities starting from the platforms themselves, focusing on design elements that create a "space of possibility" separate from the money economy: users do not think of their labour as labour, but rather as a form of play.[57] Platform owners design these platforms with an eye, above all, to galvanizing user activity, which they may use to sell attention, advertisements, and user data. As the adage goes, "On the Internet, if you aren't buying a product, you are the product."

Finally, below all of this activity – under the attention-grabbing theatrics of free and barely paid labour – runs another industry: the database marketers, data miners, and host platforms who, working under the stage and in the wings, convert the activity of writers and readers into capital. When users interact with a platform online, the platform can collect data about their activities to sell to advertisers. Advertisers, in turn, pay to display ads on the site or target users with personalized ads on other sites.[58] This layer of the online economy of textual circulation, which sees to it that not only writers but also readers add direct value to the product in the form of data, is both highly profitable and nearly omnipresent.[59] One commentator notes of a leading database marketer, "Acxiom alone has accumulated an average of 1500 pieces of data on each person in its database, which includes 96% of Americans."[60]

Is this situation so different from, say, Kernan's description of the old Grub Street, where crowds of "scribblers" scraped up a meagre income by churning out "the copy needed to fill the insatiable printing machine"?[61] For one thing, Web 2.0 is more insatiable. It demands productive labour from its participants in every facet of their lives – work, play, or otherwise – and its operations quietly but relentlessly extract it from them. For another, the new content machine is more flexible, incorporating many different ecosystems of voluntary production that prioritize playing, working, auditioning, giving, and all manner of activities in between. The writers, artists, and videographers who churn out product for content farms for a pittance, the journalists who give free copy to brand-name platforms in exchange for exposure, the actors who produce original shows for YouTube in the hope of making a living on the advertising revenue, belong to a more demanding, and less certain, economy of labour than Grub Street's scribblers ever did.

Moreover, the new content machine is more prolific. The most ink-splattered writers of the great age of print would be hard-pressed to match the output of some of the teenage girls who contribute to fan fiction sites today. One result of this situation is a textual abundance that commentators have theorized endlessly in terms of "information overload" – and, concomitantly, new methods of information management, many of which rely, like content production, on the voluntary labour of users.[62] Another result is a new practical understanding of the text, as I suggested above, in the terms of a living entity. A full account of the forms and functions of letters in this "brave world of new media" has yet to be written, but we are already beginning to register the shocks of the changes that have passed through. Are the rewards of such changes enough to compensate for the loss of other rewards – notably, the traditional forms of credit and payment that belong to print culture? At present, it is too soon to tell. But for critics, they offer at least the excitements of shifting repertoires and new horizons of meaning.

# 2

# The Republic of Games

This chapter uses tools and frameworks from game studies to examine content production on social media. Focusing on Facebook, I show how social-media platforms utilize game mechanics – including feedback in the form of scoring mechanisms, systems of rules, and a bounded environment – to engage users, and how reference to these mechanics can help us to better understand the economy of free labour that is thriving in the digital environment. I also explore the relationship between the gamification practices that have thrived online and the reader's distinctive role as a fulcrum of design for the webpage. The game economy that I identify in these textual ecosystems does not apply to print culture because print culture lacked the constellation of properties that constitute a minimal definition of a game; many social-media platforms have adopted this constellation of properties in order to keep the reader perpetually engaged in the activities of reading, navigating, and adding to the body of the text.

## 1

I will begin by discussing the controversy, within game studies circles, surrounding the concept of "gamification." A number of people in game studies, most notably the game scholar Ian Bogost, challenge the idea that the addition of a set of simple mechanics to an activity can turn it into a game. By addressing the controversy head-on, I hope to establish a foundation for using gamification as a descriptive concept for an observable and widespread phenomenon in social media. The summary is that, first, I have chosen to use a minimal definition of game, since comparative statements about high- and low-quality games are irrelevant to this discussion; and, second, I am speaking descriptively, not prescriptively. The addition of (for example) points mechanics to social-media microsystems is an undeniable fact of our current "digital condition"; the historical fact of this addition is indifferent to the question of whether these mechanics make the resulting texts more artistic, more sophisticated, or more effective in galvanizing personal or social change.

Ian Bogost has been perhaps the most vocal opponent of the concept of gamification. In recent years, he has published a number of widely cited blog posts (many critiques of gamification have taken the form of blog posts) that describe gamification as a misleading and even dangerous concept. These posts make his position on the subject clear; one is titled, simply, "Gamification Is Bullshit." He uses the term bullshit with reference to the philosopher Harry Frankfurt, who defines the term, Bogost suggests, by the fact that "bullshit is used to conceal, to impress or to coerce."[1]

But Bogost's gloss of Frankfurt's definition is inaccurate. Frankfurt uses the term bullshit to refer to statements about which the speaker doesn't care whether they are false or true. Both lies and the truth can be used to impress or coerce. There can be no doubt that gamification is a real phenomenon, heavily documented in industry discourse and practice; the fact that the term is being used to impress and coerce, which it no doubt is in marketing circles, has no effect on the truth value of the claim that gamification describes an existing practice that platform owners find useful.[2]

Like many opponents of the concept of gamification, Bogost hitches his criticism to the popularity of the term in industry. He writes, "The rhetorical power of the word 'gamification' is enormous, and it does precisely what the bullshitters want: it takes games – a mysterious, magical, powerful medium that has captured the attention of millions of people – and it makes them accessible in the context of contemporary business." As such, he argues, the word has "everything to do with rhetoric, and nothing to do with games."[3] Yet as I discuss below, there is no reason to suppose that the concept of gamification, which has always been defined as *the imbrication of game elements into other kinds of activities*, has "nothing to do with games."[4] I want to avoid tautology in this discussion; I want to avoid saying that gamification must involve games because games are part of its definition. But the fact is that when Bogost, in this passage, uses the word games, he means something more than simply games: he means the kind of games that he discusses in his 2007 book *Persuasive Games*, which are serious, sophisticated, and semantically rich.[5] Recourse to tautology can at least remind us that games include games of all kinds, just as sentences include both corporate jargon and the artistic confections of Proust.[6]

Bogost's use of the word game in a sense that implies that what is being referred to is actually a special kind of game – a high-quality game, a game worthy of serious academic attention – is an instance of a tendency in the rhetoric against gamification to flirt with the No True Scotsman fallacy. The first man says, "No Scotsman eats haggis." The second man replies, "But I'm a Scotsman, and I eat haggis." The first man says, "No *true* Scotsman eats haggis." Bogost notes that people with a stake in the respectability of game play have "critiqued gamification on the grounds that it gets games wrong, mistaking incidental properties like points and levels for primary features like interactions with behavioral complexity."[7] Thus he counters elsewhere the promises of the writer Gabe Zichermann, who has proposed that we can gamify the consumer experience through "key game mechanics, such as points, badges, levels, challenges, leaderboards, rewards, and onboarding," by excluding these mechanics from his definition of true games: "Note how deftly Zichermann makes his readers believe that points, badges, levels, leader boards, and rewards are 'key game mechanics.' This is wrong, of course – key game mechanics are the operational parts of games that produce an experience of interest, enlightenment, terror, fascination, hope, or any number of other sensations. Points and levels and the like are mere gestures that provide structure and measure progress within such a system."[8]

I have chosen to use a minimal definition of games precisely to avoid this kind of rhetoric, which seems to me to resemble an argument that only a great novel is really a book. The core undertaking of this book – examining the consequences of the introduction of game mechanics to social-media platforms – requires us only to verify that these mechanics help to produce game systems, not that they help to produce game systems that pass any subjective test of value. This undertaking does not require that we make value judgments about the fact that platform owners are using these mechanics for their own benefit, nor does it require us to ask whether interest, terror, fascination, hope, or other sensations emerge from the experience of playing the resulting games. It only requires that we ask whether they *are* games. Is a game usefully defined as a system that gives us the sensations of terror, hope, and so forth? If so, then what separates a game based on the novel *Ulysses* from the novel *Ulysses*?[9]

In short, my approach in this book to the practice of gamification is descriptivist rather than prescriptivist; my interest lies in whether the phenomenon is taking place, not whether it should be taking place. The issues of whether producing game structures that work as effective instruments of storytelling, emotional expression, or policy discussion is easy or difficult; of whether popular methods of gamification favour shallow metrics like points over more sophisticated methods of setting winning conditions; and of whether corporate gamification is pernicious because it replaces real life with a magic circle[10] have no immediate place in the discussion that follows. I want to avoid these concepts of relative quality and focus, instead, on the structural transformation of social-media platforms to incorporate game systems. To that end, I explicitly treat points, badges, and the like as "key game mechanics," since they – and not emotional experience – produce the features that I treat as parts of the minimal definition of a game.

This chapter argues that the introduction of these mechanics to social-media platforms has produced not mere interactive environments, but distinctive structures of interactive play – what Espen Aarseth and Makku Eskelinen have discussed in terms of "configuration."[11] Margaret Robertson, who has complained that gamification "takes the least essential aspects of games and presents them as the most essential," has proposed that we replace the term with the unflattering term pointsification, which would highlight the most obvious method by which industry seeks to transform other kinds of activities into games. Her observation that this method is ubiquitous is accurate, and this chapter will devote space to user activities that amount to a competition for points; but since I am not excluding methods of producing minimal game structures other than the addition of points, gamification seems to be the better term to use.

## 2

Despite the mixed reception that the concept of gamification has received within game studies, the practice of gamification has helped to raise the visibility of game studies as a discipline. In recent years, the discipline of game studies has grown rapidly on the trellises of sophisticated and intellectually serious games that game makers in both industry and academia, eager to confirm the place of their art in a cultural pantheon that already enshrines film and literature, have produced. But the discipline has also grown in response to the growing economic dominance of games in our culture, reflecting a time when video and computer games together represent a multi-billion-dollar industry.[12] The interest that the corporate world has taken in games – an interest that is no doubt as self-serving as Bogost suggests – both acknowledges this economic dominance and increases the perceived relevance of scholarship that examines games, as industry and academia alike seek to better understand how games captivate audiences. Today, games have crept into the most mundane pockets of daily life via social media, mobile apps, and amusements tied to commercial brands – a phenomenon that the term gamification was coined precisely to describe.

In the early decades of game scholarship – say, from the 1950s to the 1980s – the scholars who wrote about games often worked within other humanities disciplines, and in a cultural context in which computer games, for example, entailed simpler suites of mechanics. As a result, these scholars took special interest in the dividing line that separates games from other entities. Merely to be studying games was a new enough practice that a minimal definition of a game was merited. However, even these disciplined definitions were apt to display points of difference, reflecting the fact that games are protean entities; Ludwig Wittgenstein used the game as an example of an entity that can never be defined in a way that entirely excludes exceptions to the usual rules, but only circled with definitions that share a general "family resemblance."[13]

In 1988, Bernard Suits gave games perhaps their most concise definition, describing a game as "a voluntary effort to overcome unnecessary obstacles."[14] More recently, Katie Salen and Eric Zimmerman built on his ideas to define a game more comprehensively as "a system in which players engage in an artificial conflict, defined by rules, that results in a quantifiable outcome."[15] The artificiality of the conflict is important because it separates the game from the world of consequence, allowing the players to adopt an attitude of "as if"; the rules establish a coherent separate world, give the players roles and tasks, and set conditions for inventiveness.

In the interest of clarity and precision, I will base my discussion on the six-point definition that Roger Callois proposed in 1955. While remaining a minimal conception of what makes a game, his definition has the virtue of granularity; we can check our objects against his definition piece by piece, but we can also better see, and therefore account for, liminal areas. Callois argues that six "properties" need to be present to make an activity a game: it needs to be voluntary, have boundaries in time and space, have rules, have un-predetermined winners, produce nothing useful in practical terms, and possess a sense of self-sustained separation from reality.[16] In what follows, I will adhere to a slightly loosened version of Callois's list – slightly loosened because I am willing to accept the absence of any one property. This definition has the advantage of being simple yet flexible. It sets limiting terms that most game scholars observe, such as winning conditions (a game must have un-predetermined winners); but, since it allows variations on single properties (a rule that abides by Wittgenstein's observation that a game cannot be defined in a fully exclusive sense), it can accommodate exceptions that fail to meet the full checklist but that a reasonable person would describe as a game. For example, *Tetris* does not have an outcome; eventually, the player must simply quit playing. Therefore, it arguably lacks winning conditions, since nobody wins *Tetris* once and for all. Yet intuitively, we understand that *Tetris* is a game, despite the lack of a final victory; a loosened application of Callois allows us to act on this intuition.[17] Another example of a game that lacks one of these properties is a bet – which may have no boundaries in space and time, but which most people would intuitively describe as a kind of game.

Activity on Facebook can be matched with these properties fairly directly. To begin with, activity on Facebook is clearly voluntary. Second, it produces nothing useful in practical terms.[18] Third, it has spatial boundaries: Facebooking happens at the web address "www.facebook.com" and not elsewhere. Moreover, real boundaries delimit the virtual spaces that constitute websites; different platforms display different layouts, host different communities of users, and maintain different rules of play.

Briefly describing the virtual space of Facebook can help to establish that the platform circumscribes a self-sustained alternate world – what Callois calls a "second-order reality," and what Johan Huizinga calls a "magic circle." Moreover, a description of the platform's interface can help to make clear the importance that the platform accords to fostering extensive user engagement, which provides useful context for understanding the platform's adoption of game mechanics. On the home page, tabs at the top and along both sides of the page display navigation elements and nested items: a search bar, navigation tabs ("Edit Profile," "Your Posts," "News Feed," "Messages," "Events"), trending news stories, nested ads, nested profile pictures of "People You May Know," and so on. Clicking on any of these items leads to a new page with a new set of tabs and navigation elements. At the upper centre of the home page – the most prominent place on the page – resides a white box-shaped space (which Facebook calls the publisher or the share box) and, inside it, an invitation to write: "What's on your mind?" The layout gives the second most prominent place on the page, a vertical column down the centre of the page, to a news feed of friends' posts. In all, the layout is best described as a nested series of entry points, which enables users both to find specific content (for example, to check up on exes, a practice ruefully called Facebook stalking) and to lose their way deliberately in the labyrinth.[19]

This nested, hermetic layout encourages users to roam from place to place. It also departs from the conventions of organizing the page – and therefore the tacit instructions for use – that belonged to such mighty institutions of print as the newspaper (and indeed printed facebooks, which colleges once published to help incoming students better learn the names and faces of their classmates).[20] The layout conventions of newspapers prompt readers to treat the content in terms of a hierarchical ordering from more to less important stories, and by extension to read with a mind to the efficient use of their time.[21] The most important stories appear on the front page above the fold; slightly less important stories appear on the front page below the fold; stories that the editors have judged to be unimportant appear in the back of the paper (buried in the back of the paper, as reporters bitterly say). By contrast, Facebook promotes the novel and the winning. Facebook's layout tells users that the placement of items on the page results from two factors. The first is time: new items take precedence, being always near the top of the home page and personal profile pages. Second, popularity: items that receive many likes, shares, and comments, which Facebook's algorithms then rank higher, are displayed more prominently on the page. This aspect of Facebook is impossible to avoid, since below each post appear numbers that indicate the total likes, shares, and comments it has received: a scorecard that the writer and readers of the post can interpret to whatever end they deem appropriate.

In short, Facebook's interface design registers a profound need to encourage continual user activity. A direct sign that the site means for users to linger is that, both on the "home" page, which is a newsfeed of posts by and about the user's friends, and on the profile pages of individual users, the content is organized from newest to oldest; this implies that the user is meant to visit often, in which case the latest posts will be of greatest interest. The features that encourage users to linger include the ability, through liking, commenting, and sharing, to receive continual feedback on one's own contributions and engage with the contributions of others; to create new navigational paths and forums for user activity via user tags and hyperlinks; and to create and share items in a variety of media forms that includes videos, audio, and images. These features encourage use of the site in an exploratory, undirected manner that Kenneth Goldsmith has described as "wasting time on the Internet," with the user roaming from post to post and from profile to profile.[22] Moreover, the presence on the Facebook "page" of multiple columns of text (a main feed of posts in the center, links on the right and left to trending news stories, apps, messages, and so forth), as well as various tabs and buttons to the top, right, and left of the page, encourages users to spend time exploring the space of the page.[23] Every time the page is refreshed, the feed of posts changes, creating a new space for users to explore. This feed reflects outcomes from the infinite contest for points: the number of likes and comments that a post receives will move the post higher or lower according to the algorithm that sorts and displays feeds.

We can find formal systems of rules on Facebook at the level of constraints imposed by code, as both Galloway and Lessig have discussed in broader new-media contexts.[24] But a more interesting expression of the game structure's rage for formal constraint appears in the higher-order systems of play that users build atop the ground conditions of play that the site's protocols establish. As any regular Facebook user will recognize, the connective (shared, liked) circulation of content on Facebook takes place within a theatre of rituals and rule-bound games that users create among themselves. Consider the rituals we have built around hashtags. Clicking on a word that incorporates a hashtag brings the reader to a feed of posts that include the same hashtag. We have come to treat these feeds as forums: as prompts for jokes, stories, pictures, and even discussions of specific topics (popular hashtags on Facebook in 2015 included #LoveWins, #BlueandBlack, #Whiteand-Gold, #PrayForParis, and #BlackLivesMatter).[25] Or again, certain born-digital genres (the selfie, a concept that has engendered new genres of self-portraiture), hashtags (#TBT and #FBF for "Throwback

Thursday" and "Flashback Friday," weekly occasions for Facebook users to post old pictures), or memes (any example I gave would already be outdated) have become genres of exchange that invite constant new productivity.[26] Writing communities in the past have imposed creative constraints on themselves, but here even the creation of creative constraints is supercharged, with new examples appearing by the week. These activities have a ritual, highly structured character, as users exchange prompts and responses within a horizon of expectations set by the creative constraints of these digital genres and the traditions of the platform.

The feature that brings activity on Facebook decisively into the realm of games is, not coincidentally, Facebook's most-discussed feature: the "like" button. I will examine this feature (and others, like the "share" and "comment" buttons, that seem to be structurally similar) primarily in the light of two related game concepts: points and feedback. Points are a common, though not obligatory, feature of games because they are a simple means to obtain an obligatory feature of games: relative winners and losers, which points establish by creating measurable outcomes. We can describe likes on Facebook as points because the site treats them as points: a scoreboard under each item shows the number of likes the item has earned.[27] Shares and comments are similar; they constitute not only publishing mechanisms, but also scoring mechanisms by which users earn points. The accumulation of likes, shares, and comments can be considered a winning condition, not least because high scores can raise the visibility of a text in the platform's page ranking and search algorithm. The points that a Facebook post receives produce value as game points do, being useless outside of the space of the game yet desirable nonetheless; stories abound of people wheedling their friends to like their posts on Facebook, and myriad websites offer tips on how to boost one's likes and comments.[28] Indeed, our implicit understanding of these practices as constituting a game, even if we do not consciously recognize them as such, can be seen in the familiar praise for producing a certain kind of outstanding content: "You won the Internet."[29]

The one box on Callois's checklist that Facebook may fail to check is that of temporal boundaries. But this is not an insuperable problem; we can solve it in one of two ways. One is to dismiss the problem as irrelevant, since we have chosen, following Wittgenstein, to allow ourselves modest flexibility in our application of the checklist. Temporal boundaries are absent from many games, for example baseball, chess, and certain kinds of bets. A better solution, however, is to appeal to James Carse's distinction between finite games, which have an outcome, and infinite games, in which the objective is to prolong game play indefinitely. In these terms, we can view activity on Facebook as an infinite game. Competing against themselves and each other within a diversified point system of scoring, users create and respond to posts in an ever-shifting arena, using conventional tropes of social media, some of them quite recent inventions (the word selfie dates from 2002), as pretexts or occasions to create new content. These tropes of production and response (post a selfie; post a video of your friends performing a popular dance; post an old photograph with the hashtag #TBT; post an image of three fictional characters you identify with; tell us what colours you see when you look at "the dress") function, in part, as voluntary obstacles: as rules of play. The textual culture is sociable, fluid, improvisatory, and immediate; writers are always, in a sense, in the immediate company of other writers. There is no "winning" Facebook once and for all; rather, the objective of playing is to continue the game.

How do players sustain a sense of progress in an infinite game, since it never reaches the closure of a final outcome? Jane McGonigal answers this question by citing the concept of feedback, or external measures of player progress. Points are just one kind of feedback, just as a Labrador is one kind of dog.[30] Many infinite games combine multiple kinds of feedback: *Tetris*, for example, provides feedback in the form of points, which are given when a row is achieved; the visual effect of a row disappearing when it is achieved; and a rise in the difficulty of the game play as the player progresses. The experience of "realtime feedback" in an infinite game can be compelling. McGonigal comments: "On the face of it, this doesn't sound very fun. What's so compelling about working harder and harder until you lose? But in fact, *Tetris* is one of the most beloved computer games ever created – and the term 'addictive' has probably been applied to *Tetris* more than to any single-player game ever designed. What makes *Tetris* so addictive, despite the impossibility of winning, is the intensity of the feedback it provides."[31]

On platforms like Facebook and Twitter, the points systems of likes and shares provide a form of feedback much like that of *Tetris*. A player cannot arrive at a designated upper limit of points, as he could, for example, while playing Blackjack (21 points) or H.O.R.S.E. (an opponent makes five misses). Instead, the steady flow of feedback (eight people liked my last post; twenty people liked my last post) keeps the player working to maintain a satisfying state of game play, perpetually gauging his performance within the system. One could say that in this case, a winning state is not a final outcome, but rather what the player experiences as an optimal state of play. Moreover, the immediacy of feedback on these platforms is a common feature of games on digital systems, where a tight loop of feedback between player and system helps users to feel immersed in the game world.[32]

What is important to keep in mind is that unwinnable feedback systems of this kind are an entirely normal feature of games. They remind us that the pleasures of games don't always rely on a goal at the buzzer, a podium, a trophy: "The popularity of an unwinnable game like *Tetris* completely upends the stereotype that gamers are highly competitive people who care more about winning than anything else. Competition and winning are not defining traits of games ... Many gamers would rather keep playing than win – thereby ending the game. In high-feedback games, the state of being intensely engaged may ultimately be more pleasurable than even the satisfaction of winning."[33]

By keeping users engaged in the act of play, feedback systems correspond with a wider suite of devices with which Facebook aims to keep users glued to their devices. It is in this sense that the textual condition of Facebook promotes an aesthetic of liveness and immediacy. The users of Facebook conduct public conversations with one another, simulating the immediacy and quick turns of oral exchange; they direct their reading according to what's "new," a necessity created by the fact that the site organizes the feed from newer to older content; and they incorporate new events (recent comments, recent "reactions," breaking news stories) into their contributions. This suggests a set of practices and expectations on the part of users that emphasize sociability, improvisation, and immediacy of response (which is to say virtual presence). These are practices that belong more to theatre, conversation, and game play than to (for example) the archives and libraries that anchor the old culture of print, which are based on forms of communication other than live or near-live performance, and which therefore observe a considerably longer temporal horizon. As I have mentioned, message boards and social-media sites where users rarely post are referred to as "dead." This is not the case for library archives; even the dustiest corner of the Vatican archives is understood as the residence of a living past.

The relationship between Facebook's activity-driving mechanics and its status as a new kind of "page" is not accidental. A major difference between the digital page and the print page is the role that the reader's presence plays in its design and functioning. The metrics that we use to measure the success of websites, such as traffic, average time on the site, bounce rate, and so on, require that users spend as much time as possible inside the space of the site, which is not the case for printed texts. If I publish a book, it doesn't matter to me or my publishers whether you, as a reader, memorize a given page at a glance, read at a more measured rate, or spend hours poring over it letter by letter.[34] If I create a website, it absolutely matters whether the users spend seconds or hours on each page. This is a significant difference between literary architectures based on print – such as libraries, books, and archives – and the digital platforms that borrow from their design elements (the look of a webpage, for example) and terminology (the word page itself). The introduction of time, user presence, and interactivity as significant operating characteristics of these platforms obliges us to see them within a new framework of media analysis.

It is true, of course, that an unread book and an unread webpage can be said to share the same ontological status in that both exist. But an unread webpage very often soon ceases to exist. There is no reason to keep a site around if nobody visits it; the expenses in site maintenance, support staff, and so forth are too high.[35] In fact, the metrics of success for websites – such as traffic, on which advertising revenue hinges, and bounce rate, a measure of the average amount of time users spend on a website – make it important that users spend time lingering over the text. Print media, by contrast, has no such requirements. The material conditions that subtend websites – sometimes forgotten in the mythologizing rhetoric of cyberspace, the virtual, and, more recently, "the cloud," which provides the Web with a Romantic landscape of pure spirit – establish an unusual set of temporal boundaries by creating a necessity for users to linger over and return often to the space of the page. This condition of digital media is precisely what has led to the incorporation of game mechanics into the social-media platforms. Social-media platforms that include game mechanics – not only Facebook, but also Twitter, YouTube, Tumblr, Foursquare, and Digg, among other examples – do so in the pursuit of high traffic and lingering usage. They are designing for their very existence, for – to modify a quotation by Alexander Galloway – a website, like a game, may be said only to "exist when enacted."[36]

## 3

Van Dijck underlines the importance of the interdependence of new-media platforms. Facebook enjoys such a dominant position in the attention economy of the Web not only because it is a widely used platform – as of 2013, more than 70 per cent of adults with access to the Internet used Facebook – but also because features of other platforms take Facebook's functionality into account.[37] YouTube provides a "share" button that allows users to instantly share videos on Facebook. News publishers who work for the online instantiations of old-media giants seek out information about the algorithms that rank stories in Facebook's news feed in order to improve the chances of their stories trending on Facebook.[38] Moreover, equivalents of Facebook's famous "like" button – buttons for assigning points to items on sites ranging from Twitter to YouTube, and consequently for setting content production into a competitive context – pervade the social-media ecosystem. These scoring mechanisms produce measurable outcomes that hold meaning only within the boundaries of their respective platforms; yet they also contribute to a common culture, independent of any specific platform, of competitive play under similar terms. Van Dijck identifies these parallel social and technological architectures as a key feature of what McGann calls our "digital condition": "What characterizes the [online media] ecosystem most is the *interdependence* and *interoperability* of platforms … Buttons for sharing, trending, following and favoriting are distinctly different, but they also share a common logic; the ubiquitous implementation of a competing platform's button signals not just a technological alignment but a strategic maneuver to boost user traffic and infiltrate user routines. For instance, the integration of Twitter's 'trending' button in many platforms as well as traditional media such as television news and entertainment profoundly influences journalists' professional practices and user habits."[39]

We engage, then, in parallel play in parallel virtual arenas. Increasingly, the institutions that dominated the great age of print are "technologically aligning" themselves with the scoring mechanisms of social media; *The New York Times*, for example, has added buttons to its website that allow readers to share stories on Facebook, Twitter, Pinterest, and other social-media sites. Even literary production increasingly takes place within this republic of games. In chapter 3 I will discuss fan fiction sites, which, although their users represent a narrow demographic, are major scenes for the production and circulation of amateur fiction, with some sites "challeng[ing] Facebook in the amount of time spent browsing within the domain." These sites, too, can be defined as social media, since their major functions include hosting online communities.[40] Any Internet user can recognize the distinctive suite of rules and rituals – whimsical to some, hermetic or frivolous to others – that have arisen on digital networks as distinctively digital forms of audience activity: screencapping, remixing, role-playing, creating imitations, subjecting to "Internet famous" in-jokes.[41]

The media scholar Ethan Zuckerman has summarized this set of practices with a famous quip: "Web 2.0 was created to allow people to share pictures of cute cats."[42] The phrase Web 2.0 refers largely to social media; his examples include YouTube, Flickr, and Twitter. "Cute cats" stands in here for the Buzzfeeding, blooming confusion of shallow but entertaining content production; at the time of this writing, popular memetic items on the Web involving cats included videos of cats being frightened by cucumbers; animated images of a cat with a pop-tart for a body; and the grandfather of them all, "lolcats," which are image macros of cats which have been superimposed with comedic text. What is important to note about this form of content production – which is also a form of content reception, since these rubrics are often overlaid onto works from other media – is that it is derivative, a term that I use descriptively and without value judgment.[43] Memetic production entails imitation; it entails a crowd of people who derive, then apply, a set of rules to produce something creative. The term meme comes from Richard Dawkins, who defines a meme broadly as "a unit of cultural transmission, or a unit of imitation." More recently, it has gained an additional, narrower definition – in the context of the Web – of derivative imitations of a famous image, text, or video.[44] The importance of rules to this form of audience activity – or, more precisely, to establishing a context of competitive play that drives up user-generated content – may be seen in the ubiquity of hashtags on Facebook and Twitter that entail the sharing of rules and then the production of content within them. #FBF: post a picture of yourself from the past. #FirstSevenJobs: post a list of your first seven jobs. New examples appear every day.

Jesper Juul identifies the establishment of simple rules, then the building of higher orders of play upon them, as the oldest and most common game structure. "Emergence is the primordial game structure, where a game is specified as a small number of rules that combine and yield large numbers of game variations for which the players must design strategies to handle. This is found in card and board games, in sports, and in most action and all strategy games."[45] Since Callois includes the presence of rules as one of his six properties of a game, an account of social media in terms of game mechanics would be incomplete without recognizing the contribution that rules make to the experience of social media. I discuss the place of rules in cultures of user-generated content further in chapter 3. As many scholars have discussed, the interface architectures at the front end of websites and the protocols and programs at the back end constitute unambiguous rules that constrain what users can do.[46] Given this, it is notable that the culture of social media so enthusiastically embraces new systems of productive constraint. And how do we know when a user has produced content that displays competent play within these rules (or – perhaps – *beautiful* play within these rules, creatively working around them to seize upon a possibility that nobody else has noticed?)? The point systems that scorecard beside the posts track are seen to display audience judgments of success. Successful posts earn enough likes for their scorecards to display a visible measure of relative success compared with other posts, for whatever that's worth – nothing in economic terms, but something in symbolic and emotional terms; some of the world's biggest digital content providers are counting on it. They earn enough likes to climb via ranking algorithms; they earn enough likes, shares, follows, favourites, and retweets to go viral. They win the Internet.

All of this is by way of seeking to add a few terms to our understanding of the free labour economy online. The triumph of social media – the economic success of Facebook, Twitter, and similar platforms – relies profoundly on the free contributions of users: a reliance that is, even now, something of a mystery and an embarrassment. Indeed, as Antonio Ceraso suggests, the question of how to explain and exploit prosumers, or users who consume and produce as part of the same activity, has become a veritable industry among technology critics, with no ready consensus in sight.[47] Chapter 1 discussed the long shadow, in this literature, of Barbrook's concept of a "hi-tech gift economy," which ultimately relies on the intrinsic desire to give – combined with opportunity, that is, greater leisure time in industrialized societies: "By working for money during some of the week, people can now enjoy the delights of giving gifts at other times."[48] More recently, Clay Shirky has appealed to a similar explanatory model: the "unstructured time cumulatively available to educated populations," which once went into passive entertainment such as films and television, has moved into spaces of (inter)active entertainment online, adding up to "billions of collective hours per year."[49] As for why we give so freely in these new spaces, Shirky suggests we obey "intrinsic motivations ... fundamental to human nature": the desire to master subject matter, the desire to belong to a group, the desire to connect with others.[50] However, Ceraso persuasively argues that Shirky's claim is ahistorical.[51] Why have we built, at this moment, a free labour economy that so far exceeds the potlatch in both scale and scope?

The spread of gamification practices online has given some historically distinctive features to free content production in our era. If once we could claim to belong to a cyber-utopian gifting culture, now we must acknowledge the intrusion into the networked world of other structures of amusement. *Why* people play is an unanswerable question with claims on many fields, which is why we tend to treat the question as less important than the fact *that* we do it, that it holds for us an intrinsic appeal: that play feels to us like play. But we can at least find a historical point of distinction in the imbrication of points, rules, magic circles, and winning conditions into the "ever-expanding ecosystem of connective media."[52] To that extent, the world of social media can be seen to operate not as a gift economy, but as a game economy.

It is important to keep in mind that game mechanics are only a contributing portion of a larger suite of "persuasive design techniques" on social-media platforms designed to keep users returning and contributing.[53] Even the central application of these platforms – providing a social habitat – is carefully delivered in ways that prolong user activity. Some social-media platforms allow users to create login accounts under pseudonyms; others not only encourage the use of pseudonyms, but actively demand that users not disclose information from their "real" identities; Facebook is usually strict about enforcing a connection between profile pages and "real" identities.[54] Still, regardless of their rules about identity, social-media platforms are generally alike in their strategy of building user investment by encouraging users to engage in identity display and find validation within social groups. By encouraging, and at times requiring, users to build personal profile pages – which display personal information and social network information, and which constitute the user's base of interaction with the community – these platforms enable users to enjoy a social experience while separating that experience from the communities they build in real life or elsewhere on the Web. In the case of Facebook, the design of the profile page heavily encourages the user to display her interests, personal relationships, religious and political beliefs, school and work affiliations, and so forth. The comments, likes, and shares that other users award to her posts reinforce her connection to the platform; they tie the user to a living community and remind her that her identity and responsibilities on the platform exist within social frameworks that are specific to that platform.[55] The distinctiveness – the stylization – of the social culture of these sites constitutes a world of play separate from the real world, liberating precisely because it *is* separate from the real world, even if our identities and social networks on these sites "overlap" with real life. The need to prolong user activity is the driving condition of these platforms; the gamification of digital culture is a consequence of that condition.

4

What difference does a view of social media that focuses on game mechanics make to our understanding of the place of amateur content creation online within the history of the "Republic of Letters"? In the next chapter I will suggest, based on a look at a major digital platform for writing and circulating fan fiction, that a game studies view may help us to understand the ways in which the activity of these writers differs from authorship within what Alvin Kernan calls the "romantic print-based order of letters" without taking recourse to the technologically deterministic explanation that writing in this system is different simply because it is online.[56] Much of the writing on these sites takes place outside of Romantic frames of authorship: the writing is often anonymous, the content is debatably original, and the field emphasizes response to "prompts" at least as strongly as it does the creation of new storylines. For better or worse, literary studies has often taken the production of fiction as the measure of authorial roles in a given period, and the design of these fiction forums, which share important mechanics with social-media platforms, reveals much about the ways in which we construe authorship in the digital environment. Users of these sites are authors, but crucially they are also game players.

In this chapter, I have laid the groundwork for this discussion by showing how familiar platforms for digital communication give a prominent role to game mechanics. The implications of this discussion are modest but useful, I hope. First, it offers a salutary reminder that gamification, including the much-maligned form of gamification that focuses on simple game mechanics such as points, is a real phenomenon in the world that has an effect on the architecture of popular digital platforms. Game studies should not turn away from the concept of gamification because its methods are "shallow" any more than social-movement theorists should ignore Twitter activism because it constitutes an unreliable suite of methods for effecting social change, relying as it does on "weak ties."

Second, game thinking offers new insights into the mystery of volunteer labour in the digital environment. The ethos of a gift economy may have appealed to the small population of the early Web, but a great many digital platforms appear to have turned to game mechanics, which reconfigure labour as *fun*, in order to generate free activity and free content from massive numbers of users. In the long run, this framework for understanding cultural production online may aid us in the hard work of re-theorizing the relationship between work and leisure in the digital age. E.P. Thompson, Robert Darnton, and other social historians have discussed at length the ways in which work and leisure in the pre-industrial period differed from work and leisure in the industrial period. Observing the close relationship between games and fiction production and reception in the digital environment can show us new ways to think about work and leisure in the era of prosumers, micro-economies, and social media.

The operational principles and social practices that govern some of the largest and most influential digital media platforms require, if we wish to understand them more fully, a different framework of media analysis than the frameworks we used for the major institutions of print. I have also offered reasons for turning to game studies as a useful framework for understanding these platforms. Without doubt, the game mechanics that govern these platforms are often slight compared with those of more ambitious games, corresponding to the kind of game design that Margaret Robertson labelled pointsification. Perhaps Robertson, Bogost, et al. are correct in their claim that gamification as an approach to either games or external goals – and especially the way that gamification practices often focus on game mechanics that they identify as shallow, such as points and badges – represents a pernicious trend in the commerce between game studies and the larger world. But even if the rhetoric, for whatever reason, offends our sensibilities, it corresponds with an actual practice that has a powerful effect on Internet culture. We turn away from the concept of gamification at the peril of overlooking a distinctive and influential aspect of our digital moment. In the 1980s, the words of the character Gordon Gecko – "Greed is good" – struck audiences as pernicious and yet representative of important trends in their culture.[57] In our own time, the ethos of institutions trying to succeed in the world of new media appears to be: Games are good.

# 3

# The Great Game

This chapter examines the amateur production of fiction in the digital environment, with a special focus on a specific form of amateur literary production: fan fiction. I argue that fan fiction "archives," which are the most popular platforms for the production of fiction online, take their structure from game play. To this end, I examine characteristics of fan fiction platforms that bring activity on these platforms into correspondence with a minimal definition of a game: in particular, winning conditions, a rejection of the profit motive, a bounded space of play, and formal systems of rules. The concept of a "game of literature" has, of course, seen long use as a metaphor, often in cynical reference to the intrigues of the literary profession. If we did not recognize shared elements between game play and the book business, then the *New Yorker* cover that portrays the "Literary Field" as a sports field on which aspiring writers block each other, lunge for prizes, and run pass patterns with manuscripts on their way toward the goal line would not work as comedy. In fact, metaphors that connect literary activity with game play are older than print, reflecting a rich history of social practices that use literature as an instrument in games of cultural formation: circulating verse at court, assembling the bones of an exquisite corpse, duelling with interpretations at the seminar table. Yet these contexts of competition were minor and irregular occasions in literary systems that, on the whole, adhered to commercial or gift economies. When I argue that literary activity on fan fiction sites is better understood if these sites are conceived as

game spaces rather than as traditional literary architectures, I mean
to draw a categorical distinction between the activity on these
archives and the character of most literary production in the print
and manuscript eras. An understanding of fan culture online as, in
part, a game culture, with game mechanics that reflect both the
embedded codes of specific platforms and higher-order systems of
play that users build atop these codes, can help us to better typol-
ogize the formations of genre, authorship, and audience that arise
on these sites. It can also help us to move beyond the gift as the primary framework for understanding not only fan culture, but the
cultures of free and voluntary content production that thrive on
the Web at large.

# 1

Fan fiction, a form of amateur fiction writing dedicated to world-
building and storytelling about existing media properties, is an immensely popular activity online, with major fan fiction sites "challeng[ing] Facebook in the amount of time spent browsing within
the domain."[1] Fan fiction has not attracted as many quantitative
studies as it has sociological and literary analyses; still, the blogger
Charles Sendlor's statistical analysis of a large fan fiction site,
FanFiction.net, supports qualitative evaluations of fan fiction writers as largely female, describing the site's user base as young, female, and prolific.[2] FanFiction.net is the most popular archive for
fan fiction on the Internet, with some 2.2 million registered users
as of March 2014.[3] Sendlor finds that of all the FanFiction.net
members who joined in 2010, 78 per cent are female and 80 per
cent are between thirteen and seventeen years old. On average,
each member submitted 2.9 stories that year. Sendlor found no
gender difference in the number of stories submitted. And this is
just one site of many; the roughly 300,500 stories that users submitted to FanFiction.net in 2010 should be added to the hundreds
of thousands of stories that users submitted to other sites such as
Tumblr, LiveJournal, and Archive of Our Own, which since its
launch in 2009 has acquired over one million titles. In terms of
sheer word count, it would appear, teenage girls are among the

most prolific writers of amateur fiction on the planet. What can this activity tell us, then, about the media environment that has made it so prolific a form of literary production?

Fan fiction has been the subject of a rich and growing body of scholarship in the past few decades.[4] It has especially captivated scholars of new media, who see it as a consequence of phenomena in the world of new media that raise the amateur to an equal rank with the professional and the reader to an equal rank with the author: media convergence, in which multiple delivery methods share the distribution of media content; the read-write architecture of the Web, which allows readers to comment, share, and remix content. It has also interested legal scholars who see fan fiction as an instance of the economically important "remix culture" online, and who therefore focus on whether fan fiction constitutes "fair use" of existing media properties. Thus Lawrence Lessig, for example, in a book that seeks to defend remix culture from the dampening effect of copyright laws, cites a definition of fan fiction that construes it as an active process and emphasizes its noncommercial character: "'Fan Fiction,' broadly speaking, is any kind of written creativity that is based on an identifiable segment of popular culture, such as a television show, and is not produced as 'professional' writing."[5]

My interest in this chapter is in the common frameworks that critics have used to understand aspects of fan fiction such as its free and voluntary circulation, and in the possible limitations of these frameworks. Discussions of fan fiction have tended to emphasize the amateur status of the participants; writers are seen to produce and circulate texts in a form of Maussian gift exchange.[6] As well, discussions of fan fiction have often celebrated the freedom that fan fiction offers participants to break free of cultural scripts – to turn the fixed forms of mainstream culture into terms for free play.[7] This emphasis on freedom participates in a tradition of utopian discourse about the Web that reaches back to the 1990s, when cyberspace became the object of a new gospel that promised levels of freedom and autonomy that no society had yet enjoyed.[8] Lessig recalls that, when he was teaching Internet law in the early days of the Web, "the students seemed drunk with" the promise of an Internet that no state or corporation could control.[9] While this gospel of freedom has been dampened by events in the decades since, as governments have learned to surveil Internet activity and corporations have learned to guide it using code, academic discussions of fan fiction and fan culture remain a recognizable outpost of the old utopia.[10]

The distinctive literary system of fan fiction participates in a wider set of transformations to the world of letters in the digital age. Lessig, whose interest is in the relationship between free and controlled activity in the social ecosystem of the Web, projects a future for the sharing economy in the form of "hybrid" websites that join commercial and amateur activity.[11] As the second chapter discussed, there are reasons for us to consider game mechanics to be an overlooked component of this hybridity: by rendering the free, voluntary production of content in the terms of game play, social-media platforms support a distinctive textual culture defined by continuous user activity, thus using amateur labour to support commercial ends.[12] The triumph of fan fiction as a literary form – speaking in terms of the number of texts published and the amount of time users spend on fan fiction sites – is another consequence of this set of practices. In this chapter, I examine the role of game mechanics in regulating activity on fan fiction archives, which we can regard as social-media sites that host the circulation of fan fiction.[13] As elsewhere, my account is descriptive rather than prescriptive; that is, I do not care whether game mechanics online are desirable. I only care that they have a powerful effect on amateur literary production online, enacting forms of control and constraint that challenge descriptions of fan activity in terms of gift exchange and free play.

I will begin by describing the design and mechanics of a typical fan fiction site, Archive of Our Own (AO3). The features I describe can be mapped onto many other sites of its kind: FanFiction.net, as well as Tumblr and LiveJournal, which are general social-media sites that also accommodate fan fiction communities. The writers who contribute to these sites are anonymous or pseudonymous, choosing *noms de jouer* (or perhaps more appropriately for fan fiction, so much of which is about feeling and affect, *noms de la jouis-*

*sance*) that often sound a mock-adolescent tone of romance, angst, or whimsy. Together, these writers participate in an imagined community whose rituals, in contrast to those of the daily newspaper, engender a "simultaneity" that is constantly changing.[14] The previous chapter discussed ways in which social-media platforms have been designed to promote novelty, pressing users to check out the newest stories and the latest additions to ongoing conversations; the design of fan fiction sites is no different, with the home page for each media property displaying the stories in order of the most recent update. Not coincidentally, the most popular media properties for fan fiction writers tend to be serial works, which operate on a promise of continuation that fosters audience growth and commitment: there will be more installments after this one, and the end will arrive only after the most reluctant and amorous of delays.[15]

The name Archive of Our Own alludes to feminist critical tradition, both through Virginia Woolf (*A Room of One's Own*) and, more obliquely, through a long history of counterpublics that place women at the centre of discourse, rather than the periphery; in this view, *our own* is a phrase that refers to fans, lay readers, and women.[16] Certainly, gender consciousness is an intrinsic feature of activity on the site, which self-consciously presents itself as a space of belonging for people from a range of sexual and gender identities. For example, the basic filter for stories on AO3, which sorts according to relationship categories that include "M/M," "M/F," "F/F," and "other," pointedly normalizes non-heterosexual identity. Outside numbers on the demographics of AO3's users are not available, but a survey that AO3 published in 2013 found that 80 per cent of the site's users identified as *female*; a further 16 per cent identified as transgender, androgynous, agender, genderqueer, neutrois, trans, or other.[17] Perhaps more important than the percentages themselves is that the archive fosters a community ethos that made such a comprehensive taxonomy feel necessary (or at least desirable). The breakdown of user sexualities in the same survey includes 29 per cent heterosexual, 5 per cent homosexual, 23 per cent bisexual, and varying percentages of pansexual, asexual, demisexual, grey-asexual, queer, and other.[18]

A short site description on the home page emphasizes the amateur, non-commercial, non-profit character of the site: "We're a fan-created, fan-run, non-profit, non-commercial archive for transformative fanworks, like fan fiction, fan art, fan videos, and podfic."[19] A site description is an almost obligatory part of website design, but in this case the language also has critical and legal purposes. Legally, the concept of transformation has been used in efforts to protect works that may fall afoul of copyright law. Lessig uses the term *transformative* in a quick-and-dirty way to distinguish the remix, which transforms the source material and which he seeks to protect as a creative enterprise, from the copy, which does not transform the source material but merely shares it.[20] The site description thus tacitly acknowledges that the content on the site is at risk of being challenged by copyright holders; it adheres to a different set of values from those that were set into law by the political and legal structures surrounding older media systems. Meanwhile some fan communities distinguish between affirmational fandom, which interprets and develops the source material without changing it (for example, when a fan creates layout maps of the starship *Enterprise* based on information from the show), and transformational fandom, which changes the source material (for example, when a fan writes a story about a love affair between Kirk and Spock).[21] In defining itself as "an archive for transformative fanworks," AO3 has planted a flag in this debate.

Like Facebook, the site is designed to facilitate exploration. The user is meant to linger; more than this, the user is meant to have an immersive experience. The overall design is best described in terms of a nested architecture. On the home page, a simple red tab displays a search bar, a "Log In" tab for writers, and a set of navigation tabs ("Fandoms," "Browse," "Search," "About"). Clicking on any of the tabs leads to a new set of entry points. For example, "Fandoms" leads to a set of links for theatre, film, television, books and literature, and so forth; clicking on any of these links, in turn, leads to a page with an alphabetical list of media titles (the page for the category books and literature lists "American Gods," "Anne of Green Gables," "Arthurian Mythology," and so forth. Selecting a particular media title brings the user to a separate page; there, a new search bar allows the user to call up stories that fit any number of parameters. This nested architecture encourages exploratory activity while also enabling discovery at a granular level, allowing the user either to lose her way deliberately in browsing or to find extremely specific story types. Forget the Barnes & Noble categories of Poetry, Romance, Science Fiction and Fantasy, Mystery and Crime, and so forth; on this site, you can find, if you wish, stories set in the universe of G.R.R. Martin's book series, *A Song of Ice and Fire*, that feature the character Arya Stark and incorporate world-building from Philip Pullman's book series *His Dark Materials*. You can find seven such stories, in fact.[22]

To anchor my discussion, I will use as my primary example the section of the site dedicated to the book series *A Song of Ice and Fire*. I choose this media title, first, because it is popular and has an active fandom on the site, and therefore provides a substantial body of material to work with. Second, Martin's books are at once literary works and a familiar type of source material for fandom. The media scholar Roberta Pearson has noted the curious bifurcation between the creative works we call ourselves fans of and those we describe in other ways: we are connoisseurs of Bach, buffs or devotees of Shakespeare, but fans of *Star Trek*.[23] As an acknowledgment of this bifurcation, I have chosen a media title that is categorically literature, but also belongs to a genre (fantasy) with deep roots in fan culture at large. Third, the fan community for this series is self-consciously, playfully intertextual in a way that literary scholars will find familiar; for example, discussion boards about the series often refer to the author, George R.R. Martin, as "GRRM," which is both a handy abbreviation and a nod to those other writers of the magical, the Brothers Grimm. Discussion boards about the television show based on the books refer to the showrunners, David Benioff and D.B. Weiss, as "D&D" – a popular abbreviation for the tabletop game "Dungeons and Dragons." The transferred signifier acknowledges that fan traditions for games can feed into literary fandoms as much as can fan traditions for literary works.

Finally – a minor reason, but for me a necessary one – *A Song of Ice and Fire* isn't my fandom. I have participated in fan culture (*Star Trek*) since the early days of the Web, but not as an "aca-fan" –

Henry Jenkins's term for a scholar who foregrounds their own fan experiences.[24] I am familiar with Martin's book series, and I have written a little about the languages in the books, but I approach the fan writing associated with the series as an outsider. The features that I describe are common, however, to all stories on the site.

The home page for *A Song of Ice and Fire* is the starting point for every user, new or returning. The page follows the general design of the site as a set of multiple nested entry points: to the right, a search tab that can be used to filter the stories written for this title; to the left, a list or feed of hyperlinked story titles, for which we can regard the hyperlinks themselves as another type of entry point. In fact, hyperlinks abound on the page, modifying story titles, story tags, folksonomy classifications, and author names; this heavy hyperlinking encourages exploratory use of the site, with the user wandering from link to link. As a pre-set starting point, the stories are organized by date, with the newest stories filling the home page every time the user visits; the ideal user presumably visits regularly and looks for what's new.

Jerome McGann has written provocatively about the determining role of interface in defining the "functional character" of databases.[25] The interface of AO3 draws heavily upon the bibliographic metaphor of the archive, as the site's abundant bibliographic language shows: archive, author, bookmarks, chapter. Following McGann, I describe this use of the archive concept as a metaphor because it fits imperfectly with the digital entity called by that name. The authors that populate AO3 are not authors in the sense that the literary system of print enshrined. In the language of letters, these names are anachronisms; in the language of design, they are skeuomorphisms, or outdated design elements that are present in order to help users understand a new tool's functioning. In the case of AO3, the archive metaphor is even more dubious than it is for the academic databases that McGann discusses, since AO3 does not preserve its contents indefinitely, and since it deals in copies rather than originals. In chapter 4, I will further discuss the uses of bibliographic metaphor to describe the new information regimes of the Web.

In accordance with archival prerogative, the home page for *A Song of Ice and Fire* displays information about the holdings – an analogue to the bibliographic information that library classification systems encode, although with some marked differences from what library classification systems designate as important. On the front page, the user sees information about the total number of stories belonging to this category (tens of thousands at the time of this writing); information about the title, author, ratings, and folksonomy classifications of every story currently visible on the page; and, on the search tab, information about the various categories into which stories are grouped. The level of granularity that the search filter enables is extremely fine: to give only a partial list, the user can filter stories according to the number of points received, the number of comments received, the date of creation, the characters who appear, the relationships that appear, the story's "rating," the story's "warnings" (for example, character death), and the genre categories that apply (e.g., alternate universe, crossover, drabble, drama). If these options fail to satisfy, the user can also use a search bar, typing in words and phrases that may appear in the story descriptions or story tags. Typing in the word "Oldtown," for example – the site of the books' equivalent of the Library of Alexandria – returns, at the time of this writing, twenty-six stories.

One piece of information that the site makes everywhere visible exists in no brick-and-mortar archive: points accrued. Just as, on Facebook, users can like, comment on, and share one another's posts – a scoring and feedback mechanism that creates relative losers and winners among items – on AO3, users can similarly click a button to award points ("kudos") to a story they enjoy. They can also "bookmark" the story or leave a comment on it for public view. All three of these actions will give the story a higher search rank according to the site's filter algorithms. Because they establish a competition in which individual stories emerge as relative winners and losers, these options constitute basic game mechanics.

The relationship between these game mechanics and the social practices that I discuss in the next section is complex. Yet an observable relationship maintains between them. Lessig, Galloway, Jonathan Zittrain, William Mitchell, and Joel Reidenberg have all discussed, from different disciplinary vantage points, the digital precept that "code is law": the codes of the Web, that is, the technologies that constitute the architectures of the Web, structure and regulate the activity of cyberspace, the social world that blooms and browses atop these architectures.[26] While cyberspace, like any social entity, is a dynamic set of ecosystems that comprises many (and changing) determining factors, these factors are worked out within the constraints and affordances of code. We can see an example of this relationship in the search bar that allows users to filter stories. As I discussed, the search tab normalizes non-heterosexuality by including, as a basic function, the ability to filter stories by romantic relationships that include male/female, male/male, female/female, "other," and so forth. The same values prompted the creator of the 2013 survey of AO3 users to ask about sexuality in terms of a detailed spectrum of categories. The design of the search bar reflects values, as these search categories are present due to demand; but it also creates values, as their presence teaches newcomers to the site something about the ethos of the community they are about to join.

This book has emphasized that many of the design features of sites like Facebook and AO3 are there to encourage users to "waste time" on the site. And successfully so, it would appear: users spend more than three times the hours per month on Facebook that they do on Google, and more time on Fanfiction.net, which has game mechanics similar to those on AO3, than on Facebook.[27] As a game mechanic, the point systems on these sites help to encourage users to produce more content. The "archive" of Archive of Our Own thus becomes, despite its name, not just a space for the curation of old material, but a space actively designed to generate new material. As we will see, these laws of code coexist with a rich ecosystem of socially produced game structures that have come to govern the production and reception of fan fiction.

## 2

Archive of Our Own is not anonymous, in contrast with (say) the sort of brick-and-mortar archive that gives visitors white gloves to wear when they handle the archive's contents. In those archives, once visitors have entered the reading room proper, they are anonymous and, for practical purposes, interchangeable; they work silently and leave no trace. By contrast, AO3 treats user identity in terms more akin to those of the online game Second Life, which enables users to create virtual characters that can be maintained over time, and which can be used to interact with characters controlled by other users and to explore Second Life's virtual world. In such online games, the ability to maintain an avatar, and through it to engage in social activities, is a design feature that aims to keep users returning and contributing. Journalists have profiled users who lead elaborate parallel existences through their avatars, realizing the idea (utopian from a corporate perspective, spooky from a lay perspective) of the platform as a "second life."[28]

On AO3, the users create virtual identities – login accounts under pseudonyms – for the purpose of better interacting with other users and making changes to the virtual world of the site. Users without login accounts can also award points and post comments, thereby participating in the game that these mechanics establish, but they cannot make themselves known as individuals to other users. A user with a login account can build a profile page that archives and displays information about her account: stories she has written, stories she has bookmarked, fandoms she likes, fandoms she has written for, other users who have become friends with her virtual identity. In turn, the wider community of users affirms her social existence on the site by awarding her stories points, bookmarks, and comments, which are visible on her profile page. One effect of basing the site's operations on durable virtual identities – identities that are sustained over time, but cannot be connected with the public identities of the users – is to give the users a consistent social experience in a shared space, with roles and responsibilities that rely on consistent social frameworks, that is nevertheless separate from the social worlds those users inhabit in real life, where public identity imparts a different weight of consequence. It helps to create a magic circle.

On Facebook, which also supports (indeed, insists on) the ability to maintain a profile page with a consistent identity, the requirement that the user's login identity be identical with her public identity results in a less profound separation of the user's activity from real life. Still, AO3 and Facebook are similar in their strategy of fostering user investment by encouraging users to engage in identity display and seek validation within social groups anchored in the site.[29] Profile pages on Facebook heavily promote the user's ability to display for public view her "Facebook friends," interests, religious and political beliefs, school and work affiliations, and other personal information. Profile pages on AO3 focus on the user's activity within the site, reinforcing the magic circle. In both cases, the profile page ties the user to a living community and reminds her that her virtual identity is attached to group roles and responsibilities specific to the site.

These responsibilities are more eccentric on AO3 than they are on Facebook. Consider, for example, the hermetic and politically loaded system of practices that has grown up around the technological device of folksonomy tagging. From a formal perspective, tagging is a form of information management, a method for producing user-generated metadata that can be used to search for specific categories via search filters and hyperlinks. But on AO3, tagging has become a genre of literary production in its own right. An author who publishes a story on the site must attach folksonomy tags to the story; this is a norm, not a requirement enforced by the code of the site, but deviations from this norm are rare. It is true that tagging as a practice is anchored by a rule of the site's code, which is that the search mechanism uses tags to filter stories; if an author wants her story to appear on specific search results, she must include tags consonant with those searches. But tagging as a norm entails practices that go far beyond this basic requirement, and an author who does not play by the rules can be punished through a loss of points or, at an extreme, banishment from the site. Tagging thus takes place in conformity with the technological function of tagging *and* in conformity with the social rules of the site. In what follows, I will argue for a view of this and similar practices as examples of emergence: a higher system of play that users build atop the platform's basic game parameters.

One especially prominent norm of tagging represents a whimsical rebellion *against* the strictures of code. AO3 users have developed a community practice of writing tags that are so specific or idiosyncratic that the site's search and filtering functions cannot use them. Examples of such tags from *A Song of Ice and Fire* include extremely specific plot elements (*little Theon in Winterfell for first time*), metacritical frameworks for the plot (*in which Sansa needs peace / and Jon is the way to keep the north safe*), critical evaluations of the characters (*Catelyn doesn't like children who are not her own*), reflexive comments on other tags (*Slow Burn / I guess*), and direct addresses to the readers (*I'm Bad At Tagging / Check it out though / it might be alright*). In some of these tags, the author steps forward as a kind of Shakespearean chorus, commenting on the action of the story and suggesting lessons that can be drawn from the proceedings.

Speaking purely architecturally, in terms of its function in the design of the site, the folksonomy tag section that appears above each story is not a space for this kind of open commentary. It is a space for authors to write tags that will help readers to find stories and group them under shared categories. The practice of writing tags that are self-consciously useless for this purpose is, above all, a form of satire upon (or, if you prefer, a way of playing around the edges of) the functional metaphor of the archive that gives AO3 its name and governs its interface. It calls attention to the limitations of any system of categories that might be used to organize literature, since such systems must always exclude some categories that the author or the reader feels, at least in one instance, to be relevant. In this respect, the tag sections on AO3 call to mind Borges's impossible Chinese encyclopedia, with classifications for animals that include "(a) belonging to the Emperor, (b) embalmed, (c) tame, (d) sucking pigs, (e) sirens, (f) fabulous, (g) stray dogs, (h) included in the present classification, (i) frenzied, (j) innumerable, (k) drawn with a very fine camelhair brush, (l) et cetera, (m) having just broken the water pitcher, (n) that from a long way off look like flies."[30] Such tags do not appear with all of the stories under *A Song of Ice and Fire*, but they appear with a sizeable minority.

In the course of the ongoing conversation among media scholars about the "contest," in the digital media environment, between narrative and database, one wag has asked whether there could be such a thing as a "satirical" database.[31] According to classical narratology, a narrative must follow one of a few basic genres; one of these is satire, which foregrounds the impossibility of making sense of the world using a narrative structure.[32] The question of whether there can be a satirical database is, at bottom, a question about whether the indexes that organize a database limit the arrangement of its contents in ways that block it from the critical value of narratology. The practice of whimsical tagging on AO3 provides an answer to this question: yes, there can be a satirical database, since whimsical tags, by calling attention to the inability of any set of categories to master the archive's contents, transform AO3 into just that. But because the site's search function is unable to make practical use of the tags, the result is useful only as a second-order commentary overlaid on the actual database.[33]

Another important norm of tagging concerns the unexpected. If the characters in a story fail to act in broadly predictable ways, or if the story's universe fails to conform to the rules of the canon universe, the writer is expected to flag the deviation with a tag: "OOC," out of character; "AU," alternate universe. (Tellingly, fans call the official stories "canon," a term borrowed from Biblical hermeneutics. It is well known that literary scholarship derives its ultimate genealogy from Biblical hermeneutics. Fan culture presents, as we might expect, a playful travesty of this relationship: the media property is *canon*, the comments of the media creators are *word of God*, and so forth.) Even more importantly, certain story elements that readers may want to avoid, such as sexual content, content dealing with mental illness, or the deaths of major characters, must be signalled in the story's folksonomy tags, so that readers can avoid coming across these elements unexpectedly. Examples of stories that fall within the purview of this norm but fail to observe it are vanishingly rare. The consequences of shirking this norm for a single story might include losing points, losing bookmarks, and receiving angry remarks in the story's comments section; the consequences of shirking it for a number of stories would include losing login privileges.[34]

In short, the architecture that permits folksonomy tagging has become the stage for a host of social norms that specify how, and why, a story must be "properly" tagged, which range from defining the story's genre to flagging story elements that the AO3 community has decided must be flagged, such as departures from "canon" or, more seriously, sexual content. This indicates a strong emphasis, within this creative community, on operating within social norms, conventions, and firm rules of play – rather than, say, on absolute free play or the royal right of the author to frame her story however she pleases. A traditional literary archive – designed for the preservation of physical works in print or manuscript – uses delimiting categories such as author, genre, and catalogue metadata as external tools for information management, retroactively applying these categories to works that have already been created. In the virtual space of Archive of Our Own, these same categories, which, as navigational features, are precisely what give the site the "interface metaphor" of the archive, constitute points of social solidarity, rules that structure interaction, and creative constraints imposed for the purpose of generating new work.

Tags can also establish forums for conversation and social activity. Some tags that appear with stories under *A Song of Ice and Fire* indicate that those stories were written for "Yuletide," an annual gift exchange event in which writers ask for, and produce, stories with specific plot elements. Yuletide is one of many such events, some specific to particular fandoms, others more general: "stannismonth," during which fans make art about the character Stannis Baratheon; "AryaxGendry Week," during which fans create art about the characters Arya Stark and Gendry Waters; "Inktober," during which fans create art using ink. As "holiday seasons" specific to fan culture, these events constitute another point of separation between fandom and the outside world. These events resemble the hashtag "events" on Facebook discussed in the previous chapter, encouraging users to generate content within a restricted field of action set by the community.[35] Without the tags, the writers would not have a virtual space to gather and participate in these specialized events. Their creation reflects the tendency toward production of the republic of games, which, designed to encourage the output of new content, will seize upon more and more occasions for such output.

As another example of the formative role of constraint in fan fiction, consider the treatment of genre. Folksonomy tagging is the primary method of classifying a story on AO3. My focus here is on the genres themselves, which fan scholars such as Karen Hellekson and Kristina Busse have discussed intensively.[36] What is astonishing about the treatment of genre on AO3 is how large and granular the suite of descriptors the site finds necessary for handling genre is. As a starting point, AO3 provides dozens of "canonical tags" (the site's term for tag categories that are "universal and easily understood," used for filtering and auto-complete functions) relating to genre.[37] These include both genres familiar from literary history, such as drama, fantasy, mystery, horror, and romance, and genres specific to fan fiction, such as angst, fluff, fix-it, crack, and alternate universe. One could draw up another taxonomy of generically identifiable alternate universes: crossovers, which bring together characters from more than one media property; fusions, which combine the setting of one media property with characters from another; strange minor species, like the *coffee shop* AU; and specific alternate-universe settings belonging to famous media properties, like Lovecraft's Cthulu Mythos or the Harry Potter books. There is even a taxonomy of story types that focus on the principle of using constraints to generate creativity: the *drabble*, for example, which is a story of exactly 100 words.

To be sure, all fiction receives some legibility and context from conventions. Genre is more active than retrospective; publishers use genre categories in the book marketplace, and authors take this fact into account when writing.[38] Yet the fan fiction community's attitudes toward genre differ from those of the literary marketplace in terms of both scale and process. Genre models appeal to publishers, yes, but evading genre often appeals to literary authors. (In a study of English-language books published between 1700 and 1923, and focusing on the distinction between fiction and non-fiction – and what distinction could be clearer? – Ted Underwood suggests that some *10 per cent* of books present "puzzling boundary cases" that evade categorical type.)[39] By contrast, fan fiction seeks out constraints, a phenomenon of which the proliferation of genres and microgenres is one index. If authors like to flout genre, then in an amateur publishing environment, which is not subject to the need of publishers to sell "shelves" (categories) to Barnes &

Noble, we might expect to see genre categories dissolve. Instead, they flourish. So do other constraints, as we can see with the priority that the fan fiction community gives to constraints such as adhering to the logic, timeline, and events of the canon universe; keeping the characters "in character"; and marking the story with the relevant genre tags.

The contributors to sites like AO3 devote an immense amount of time to writing within these constraints. It is not at all uncommon to see fan fiction works, whether standalone stories or collections of shorter pieces, that exceed the word count of famously long print novels. For example, the word count for Herman Melville's novel *Moby Dick* is 206,000 words; for Margaret Mitchell's *Gone with the Wind*, 418,000 words; for Fyodor Dostoyevsky's *Crime and Punishment*, 211,600 words; for J.R.R. Tolkien's *The Lord of the Rings*, 455,000 words.[40] George R.R. Martin's first novel in the series *A Song of Ice and Fire* runs approximately 284,000 words, and it is the shortest book in the series.[41] Now consider, for comparison, the word counts of a great many stories on AO3. A search on the site for individual works that exceed 200,000 words in length returns 4,524 results. More than 1,500 titles exceed 300,000 words, and more than 650 titles exceed 400,000 words.[42]

In the context of the traditional novel, these numbers are extreme; Jane Smiley lists the typical length of a contemporary novel as 100,000–175,000 words.[43] On AO3, more than 144,000 individual works run for that length.[44] This demonstrates that fan fiction writers who produce stories for sites like AO3 are capable of tremendous productivity. These writers work without pay, in an uncertain legal context, for an audience that understands itself to be peripheral to the mainstream.[45] And yet they write prolifically; the numbers above are impressive on their own, yet they don't take into account the much larger population of stories with low word counts that, added up together, constitute the productivity of an average AO3 contributor.

The best way to understand this incredible productivity, I believe, is with reference to the rules of play that fan fiction communities follow – with an emphasis on *rules*, not *play*. As we have seen, scholars who discuss fan culture and fan production overwhelmingly describe it in terms of freedom: as a safe space to rebel, innovate, subvert givens, and challenge convention.[46] But if we put this utopian rhetoric aside and consider instead the structure and operations of a fan fiction site like AO3, it becomes clear that fan fiction is a remarkably stringent form, with its operations thoroughly defined by rules and conventions. Stories generally fit within a set of predefined genres that, across different archives, retain consistent names and features: e.g., "Drama," "Angst," "Fluff," "Crack," "Hurt/Comfort." Most archives use these genres as search categories, which indicates how entrenched and widely accepted these genres are. The settings and characters, belonging as they do to existing media properties, by definition fit into (or riff on) the outlines of stories already told, which plausibly sets these elements, too, within the suite of constraints that a fan fiction author must observe.

These features help to unify fandom as a community. But they also distinguish the online production of fan fiction from previous literary systems such as the free circulation of manuscripts or the commercial publication of texts. While Jenkins and others have celebrated the ability of fans to subvert the norms of "audience activity," this theme in fan studies has always coexisted comfortably with a separate theme that emphasizes the fit of fan production into prestigious existing modes of cultural production.[47] Many scholars of fandom, perhaps concerned that the subject of their study can be perceived as *infra dig*, have described fan fiction as a form of literature in its own right, part of a rich tradition of literary appropriation and transformation stretching back to Homer.[48] Other scholars of fandom, while retaining this emphasis on tradition and literary identity, focus on practical features of fan culture such as a sense of separation from economies of capital, which has traditionally helped to define great art in imagination if not in fact. In this view, fan culture is a continuation of the past (or, equally, a continuation of an eternal present of universal patterns of human culture) in the form of what James English calls, in another context, "a symbolic economy of pure gifts."[49] For example, Karen Hellekson describes fan culture as a gift economy based on symbolic exchange: the circulation of artworks that lack value outside of a specific community serves to create an enclosed social space.[50] In both of these critical traditions, the field of fan studies draws value, in part, from its unity with the eternal order of great art, an order that makes itself known in observable features of fan culture such as the anti-profit imperative and the deliberate construction of a field of value and identity separate from that of the "real world."

Yet, given the ubiquity of game mechanics on fan fiction websites, it seems short-sighted to reduce fan fiction to the terminology of self-publishing. If we recognize some truth to Kernan's distinction, with respect to Samuel Johnson's England, between an older system of letters based on the circulation of manuscripts and a newer literary system based on print, operating concurrently with the older system but exhibiting distinctive properties from it, then we may see the distinctive properties that govern the incredible textual output of fan fiction sites as constitutive of still another textual system – one singular to the twenty-first century.[51] Although fan fiction does qualify for the label of literature, given that literature includes narrative fiction, there is value in the Kernanian move of distinguishing the new textual system from the older one on the basis of these formal properties. My interest, as I have made clear throughout this book, is in the relationship between these formal properties and the extraordinary success of this textual system in the age of digital media. The concept of a republic of games, presented as a contrast to the traditional republic of letters, has at least the heuristic value of positing structural differences from an older textual system and the taxonomic value of delineating the formal properties that seem to be pertinent: voluntary, unpaid participation; a magic circle, or (as the previous chapter discussed) a strong appearance of one; a competitive format that creates relative winners and losers, which, in the most basic and widely observed form, means a point system of competition.

In the next section, I will consider in greater detail the differences between these textual systems. Here, I would like simply to emphasize the scope of literary fandom; the textual microsystem that constitutes AO3 belongs to a broader textual ecosystem that operates across most other fan fiction sites, representing one of the largest, if least visible, segments of literary writing and publishing today. I believe that some aspects of fan culture, which after all lives partly on gamified social-media platforms, have arisen as higher elaborations of these game elements; that, to use a familiar term from game studies, they are emergent properties of the simple games that are embedded in the structures of these platforms. Certainly, a great deal of activity on these platforms seems to reflect pleasure taken in competing within constraints; users produce content within gratuitous constraints (of genre, of folksonomy, of other deliberate patterns that have become familiar features of Internet culture, such as hashtags and memes) that echo and intensify the formal constraints of the platform. The awarding of points and comments reflects a measure, however imperfect, of the user's success within the boundaries of play. I expect that these cultures of creativity will continue to expand in the digital era along with the rise of gamified platforms. In the next section, I will further discuss how these constraints differ from the voluntary constraints of (for example) genre in the textual system of print.

## 3

So far, I have given reasons for approaching the study of fan fiction within the framework of game play. This section will briefly consider game-like aspects of literary practice in the print and manuscript eras. Literary practice in these eras did share some attributes with games, especially in instances (never a dominant source of literary production) when literary production arose from contexts of competition. Ultimately, however, literary practice in the print and manuscript eras cannot be said to fit into a game framework as decisively as fan fiction does. The claim that literary culture online merely recapitulates the gift-exchange ethos of (some) previous literary cultures overlooks important novelties of the digital example. In the final section, I will consider the relationship between technological constraint and social innovation. If fiction in the digital environment is produced and received differently than it was in earlier media systems, this is both because of the technological architecture of the platforms for producing and curating this fiction and because the digital environment has given rise to new social communities.

The use of literary production in game contexts, though never mainstream, is antique and well chronicled. In the *Decameron* and the *Canterbury Tales*, people devise and trade stories as a competition to pass the time. But these stories took place in what was fundamentally a literary system based on gift exchange: the circulation of poems in manuscript or oral performance. Sometimes explicit games of literary wit produced poetic texts, but this only happened a small percentage of the time; the circulation and preservation of poetry took place most often as free exchange, or, especially as print spread, in a consumer context of buying and selling.[52] Into the modern era, games that entail literary production have continued to break into the popular consciousness; as, for example, with exquisite corpse, a Surrealist "game" in which the players pass around a piece of paper and add new lines of text to a poem without reading the previous lines. But the term game is only a figure of speech in the case of exquisite corpse, for exquisite corpse has no winning conditions. In fact, very few of the cultural activities that produced literary texts in the period up to the year 2000 have been classifiable as games. The dominant literary system has changed many times over history, but until the rise of gamified platforms online, those changes included game structures only as rare and incidental amusements. Only recently have game structures come to subtend – as they do in the media environment of the web – the production, circulation, and preservation of texts.

As chapter 2 discussed, the change that I am identifying begins with a small set of elements: voluntariness, rules, a magic circle, separation from the money economy (on the part of the user), and winning conditions. But these basic elements can give rise to complex cultural formations. We may take as one measure of the force of these formations the contrast between professional editors in the early decades of print, who sometimes took poetic texts that originated in extra-literary contexts and reframed them as narrowly literary products, and our habit of taking media texts that originated in the traditional literary marketplace (e.g., *A Song of Ice and*

*Fire*) and turning them into social games to play online: drinking games, live-tweeting, contests of wit (such as it is) through the exchange of memes, the elaborate anti-narrative game of avoiding spoilers that the whole Internet plays together as a group. All of these activities take place predominantly on gamified platforms that create winning conditions through the awarding of points.

In short, there is a difference between playing around in the realm of literature and playing a literary game. Recognizing this difference allows us to identify elements of the textual ecosystem online that we might miss otherwise. As well, recognizing points of distinction between gift exchange and exchange based on game play enables us to better contextualize fan fiction, as a form of amateur literary production on the Web, within the larger history of literary production, and also to add new features to the historical map of the relationship between literary production and media change.

Are there characteristics of the textual ecosystem of fan fiction sites that we can connect with their gamification elements? We have already seen that authorial activity on fan fiction sites is distinctive for its high productivity. Further, we can plausibly connect this productivity to the sites' gamification elements. As Katherine Fitzpatrick and others have stressed, a website requires ongoing activity if it is not to decay; and point systems, primitive as they can seem to be, exist as part of an effort by the creators of online platforms to ensure that these platforms remain spaces of action.[53] They foreground a sense of liveness that Alexander Galloway has identified (though not exclusively) with games: "without action, games remain only in the pages of an abstract rule book ... they exist when enacted."[54]

Another characteristic of the textual ecosystem of fan fiction sites is an overt celebration of jargon and inside jokes belonging to fan culture. Hellekson proposes that we view this characteristic of the fanfic community as a deliberate establishment of shibboleths based on gift exchange: "Online media fandom is a gift culture in the symbolic realm in which fan gift exchange is performed in complex, even exclusionary symbolic ways that create a stable nexus of giving, receiving, and reciprocity that results in a community occupied with theorizing its own genderedness."[55] This argument rightly emphasizes the relationship between the social ties that arise in the fanfic community and the gender consciousness that pervades its language. Certainly, the categories of gender and sexual preference that one commonly sees marked in folksonomies on AO3 (for example, terms like demisexual) require a familiarity with the gender politics of fandom that can only be acquired through experience.

But if we understand online media fandom, at least on sites like AO3, as operating within a game economy rather than a gift economy, then we can begin to theorize the rules of exchange as important mechanisms in the separation of the real world from the world that constitutes fandom as an exclusionary realm. As Juul writes, referring to video games, "The fiction, the sentiment of as if replaces and performs the same function as do rules. Rules themselves create fictions."[56] Rules that the users of AO3 follow include political rules (creating appropriate tags for content that is sexual, violent, or otherwise contentious), procedural rules (awarding points to stories that please rather than stories that displease), and hermeneutical rules (adhering to the whimsical but poker-faced demarcations of provenance and commentary that define fan reading, as when the official story is acknowledged as canon and deviations are flagged as fanon or headcanon). The result, taken together, is a distinctive and fully realized realm set aside for playing around with media texts, rather like a Talmudic college as imagined by Lewis Carroll or a library of Borges with a serious investment in social politics. This fiction, which is the performative result of adhering to a shared set of rules, unites fan culture and separates activity on fan platforms from real life, but it results from game mechanics, not (simply) the "female-gendered task of maintaining social ties."[57] Failure to observe the rules results in fewer points (kudos, likes, bookmarks, shares, new followers, and/or positive comments, depending on the site).

The creation of fiction from rules is common enough in literary culture, but the technological codification of rules changes the impact of the fiction, especially when those rules combine with winning conditions. Most fictions follow rules of some kind, for the author, the reader, or both: e.g., read from beginning to end; keep the action within a twenty-four-hour frame; fire by the third act the rifle that hangs above the mantelpiece in the first act. For communities of readers, rules of interpretation that flout the requirements of plausibility can set conditions for new kinds of engagement with texts. Earlier generations of Sherlock Holmes fans – starting in the early twentieth century! – expressed this point when they gave the name "The Great Game" to a shared fiction of their social reading activities: the pretense that the original Sherlock Holmes stories are the true reports of the historical Doctor John Watson.[58] For them, "game" was a playful term for the act of responding to texts within a fictionalized framework. As actual games, sites like AO3 turn fanciful rules into rules embedded in the operations of the platform and the interactions of the users. For example, folksonomy classifications become goalposts for the ability to identify, and perform within, the constraints of hyper-specific microgenres; to use the esoteric language and symbols of the fanfic community; and to adhere to the fanfic community's social values, an equivalent, perhaps, to knowing the different values that sanction different kinds of physical contact in hockey and soccer games, respectively. The awarding of points renders the outcome of game play, the scores achieved, as durable, if not permanent, factors in the archival presentation of the texts: the classification systems that organize the texts document the points that each text has received, and higher-scoring texts rank higher in the results of a variety of different kinds of searches on the site.[59]

Other aspects of the social culture of fan fiction seem to have arisen independently of formal game mechanics, but, through the process of emergence, have become entangled in the dynamic system of the game. For example, throughout history, most of the authors named in anthologies of poetry have been male; fan fiction writers are predominantly female. This bias seems to have begun well before the digital era; the stories that Jenkins identifies as the earliest works of fan fiction in the modern sense, which appeared in small-circulation "zines" for *Star Trek* fans in the 1960s, were written by women.[60] The gender consciousness that Hellekson rightly identifies as an ongoing concern of the fanfic community, which she describes as "preoccupied with theorizing its own genderedness," is observably present in the politics that govern folksonomy tags. Gender consciousness is not intrinsic to the technologies that subtend AO3 as a platform, but users adapted those mechanics, for example by establishing norms for tagging, to bring gender consciousness into the patterns that characterize the system. Incidentally, the site's tagging norms offer yet another example of how the users of technologies can adapt technologies to suit their own preferences. Nothing in the technology of tagging demands that users tag sexual and gender categories in careful detail, but doing so has become a tacit condition of participating in the community. Or again, nothing in the technology of tagging demands that users create a genre of metacritical parody of classification schemes; yet this genre flourishes on AO3, and indeed has become a highly visible aspect of the "symbolic realm" of the site.

Another scene of emergent play on AO3 is authorial identity. Most fan fiction sites, AO3 among them, require users to participate under pseudonyms. This requirement, as with so many proven design elements on social-media platforms, has the effect of driving up user activity. Within the magic space of the game, players can emerge as new social actors, a transformation that, research shows, can be addicting; the use of alternate identities encourages this process, although it is not essential to it.[61] Even in games in which players act under their biographical identities – hockey, for example – a player's persona can have an uneven fit with her off-rink personality. A tongue-tied person can be eloquent in the rink; a reserved person can be brutal in the rink. Pseudonymous or not, a player identity is a real identity, albeit one circumscribed by a specific field of play, and the player may find it difficult to abandon. Requiring users to act through avatars (the common term for a player persona), and moreover avatars that remain stable over time, thus keeps users returning: first, because the connection between avatar and platform keeps users who wish to retain their avatars active on the platform, and second, because the safety of a pseudonym encourages users to try out behaviours they would miss out on in real life.[62]

What makes the adoption of pseudonymous authorial personas distinctive, in the context of literary history, is that it represents a choice of the platform rather than the author. In itself, the fictionalization of identity is hardly new to literature: examples abound of literary authors, such as Geoffrey Chaucer or Samuel Clemens, who separate themselves from the personas who take authorial credit for their works. This is reflective of the ways in which game play and literary activity share terms and even overlap; game scholars have stressed that the relationship between player and avatar can be as laden, metaphorically and semantically, as the relationship between literary author and persona.[63] But the requirement on the part of the platform that users adopt non-biographical personas presents a constraint on the author's figuration of identity at the level of code. In the ecosystem of social media, a pseudonymous avatar that a user creates on a given platform is specific to that platform; there are no built-in incentives to use the same avatar on different platforms, and some built-in hindrances to doing so. The rejection by users of this form of constraint is therefore interesting. Many users have chosen to defy this "law" of technological code by establishing a connection between their avatars on different sites, either by choosing the same pseudonym on different platforms or by announcing, on one platform, the pseudonyms that apply on other platforms. This is a form of emergence in that it represents a more complex system of activity arising from simple elements, and even overcoming their built-in tendencies.

More importantly, the replication of avatars is an instance of a larger pattern by which fans carry over the moves and choices of game-play – that is, fan activity constituted as game-play – across a variety of social-media platforms. The previous chapter discussed the bridging of similar or interconnected applications across a range of platforms in the social-media ecosystem. What I am calling attention to here is the bridging, on the part of users, of higher-level systems of rule-bound play across those platforms. As long as you know the rules and the moves, you can carry over the great game of fandom on different platforms, and indeed with different media properties from different source media. I have always been astonished that after moving to a new fandom, you can continue to play the same game without missing a beat. Regardless of the media property, the moves in the game remain largely the same from one fandom to another. In this respect, the consumption of traditional media on the Web has taken on a rule-bound, game-like structure that supertends any specific platform or media object. In the case of *A Song of Ice and Fire*, for instance, fans can use structures of exchange that bridge different platforms to exchange critical analysis within competitive formats (for example, by participating on discussion forums where users give points to content); exchange distinctive fan genres of speculation, such as headcanons, within rule-bound formats (for example, numbered question-and-answer sessions: a writer posts a numbered list of questions; her readers respond by sending numbers; the writer responds by answering the corresponding questions); produce and circulate stories in move-and-countermove patterns of prompts and fills ("this is based on a Tumblr ask," a writer announces above a story on AO3); create novel media items, such as image macros and fanvids, that adhere to extremely specific micro-genres; and use tools like Fate or Cortex Plus to create and play roleplaying games. These examples illustrate the way in which the social-media ecosystem fosters the reconstitution of other media forms as games. Chapter 4 will explore the possibility that we might consider adding another structure of organization and meaning-making, *game*, to the traditional new-media "dyad" of narrative and database.

Finally, thinking about fan fiction sites as game spaces allows us to consider the issue of originality in terms less apt to trail, as critical writing on fan fiction sometimes still does, clouds of glory from Romantic conceptions of literary authorship. Of course, exuberant play within the constraints of genre is a familiar phenomenon in literature. But in the fanfic community, the norms of production and exchange often use the constraints of genre to create a situation familiar from game play: a challenge to stimulate new activity.[64] On gamified social-media platforms for the production of fan fiction, stories often come into being through the exchange of "prompts" and "fills," a practice in which users post requests for specific stories and other users post stories that fulfill the requests. This practice reflects a textual culture that thrives on constraint; as we have seen, the culture of fan fiction has given rise to incredibly specific microgenres, the names of which writers often exchange as prompts. Sometimes a collection of stories by a single author will systematically move through tens or hundreds of microgenres, as though to foreground fan fiction's creative dependence on constraint. Originality is not what gives these fictions value in the "marketplace" of fan fiction – not, at least, with respect to the invention of character, the selection of setting, or the rules of genre, which act more like game rules to be followed than like limits to exceed. The framework of a gift economy does not explain this behaviour, but the framework of a game economy does.

4

The central claim of this chapter has been that many fan fiction platforms online feature game mechanics that render user activity as a form of game play. These mechanics include voluntary participation; a magic circle; a separation from the economy of market capital; a system of rules – some embedded in the code of the site and some enforced by the fanfic community – that users must adhere to, and by which users are judged; and a point system that creates relative winners and losers among content producers. In order to show these features in action, I have focused on the platform AO3, which I treated as a quadrat sample taken from the larger community of gamified fan fiction platforms online. As chapter 2 discussed, on social-media platforms like Facebook, game mechanics represent a deliberate tactic on the part of the platform owners to encourage user activity. On AO3, game mechanics serve a number of uses; for example, the similarity of these mechanics to the workings of other popular websites helps users to navigate a familiar environment, and the point system for evaluating stories enables users to sift through prodigious quantities of textual material. Productivity-enhancing features such as feedback and (at the level of culture rather than code) productive constraint likely help fan fiction platforms to attract and sustain tremendous user activity; users produce volumes of text that often exceed the word-counts of the novels, film scripts, and so forth of the media properties that inspire their writing, and that not uncommonly exceed the word counts of famously massive print novels.

This chapter has explored some of the questions that arise from this textual condition. What can the prolific spread of this form of literary production in the digital environment tell us about the cultural and material structures that subtend the Web? Are games surrounding the production and reception of texts distinctive of the digital era, either in absolute terms or in their position in the cultural mainstream? To what extent is the "game" of fan fiction delimited by the laws of code that regulate websites? To what extent does this game reflect higher-order systems that the fan fiction community has devised? Is this phenomenon – the transformation of art into a game – limited to born-digital fan fiction, or do these digital formations have an effect on the ways in which other media, such as films and books, are read, discussed, and constituted in digital spaces? What is the relationship, on fan fiction websites, between game mechanics and design elements from older literary systems – for example, the bibliographic language of archive and author? Ultimately, the goal of this chapter has been to register a difference between the digital republic of games and older systems of literature. The effect of game mechanics on fan fiction websites suggests that communities of writing and reading on the Web are working out distinctive ways of circulating and understanding texts. As the next chapter will discuss further, the bibliographic language of interface metaphors serves as a familiar cue that helps users interact with new digital environments; but it also represents an anachronism that disguises some of the real activities that constitute the new systems of letters emerging in the digital age.

# 4

# The Printing Press as Metaphor

So far this book has examined the effects that the rise of game mechanics on social-media platforms has had on textual cultures online. These effects are complicated by the operation of these platforms in terms of multiple distinct yet symbiotic layers: most notably, a database layer at the back end, which manages the many forms of information that user activity produces, and an interface layer at the front end, which guides user activity and provides a media framework within which users may understand the platform's functions. This chapter offers a model for understanding the complexity of remediation in the platform era, when heuristic interface metaphors – which represent the function of a system by repeating design features from an older system – present distorted genealogies for digital media platforms. In particular, the narratives that surround digital media platforms often conjure a lineage that points back through bibliographic history to the rise of the printing press, a conceit that benefits platform owners by setting an aura of inevitability around the expansion of these platforms. So powerful are these narratives in the marketplace that even their critics can find themselves repeating their terms, a condition that Bourdieu theorizes in terms of *dominated dominators*. In this chapter I will examine the wider cultural conditions that have resulted in the popular paradigm by which our "revolution" recapitulates the bibliographic revolution of Gutenberg, reducing the visibility of other histories that have contributed to digital media culture. I close by suggesting how we can restore one overlooked legacy, that of games, to existing models of new media that seek to reconcile the front and back ends of new-media artifacts via the organizing structures of narrative and database.

## 1

These days, we are constantly looking for an image of ourselves in the historical past. "The first ever information revolution," begins a typical book jacket blurb, "began with the advent of the printed book, enabling Renaissance scholars to formulate new ways of organizing and disseminating knowledge."[1] A communications scholar offers a view of our place in history that has echoes in countless other publications and presentations: "At present we are witnessing an information revolution whose significance parallels and perhaps even surpasses that of the information revolution caused by the printing press in the fifteenth century."[2] Publishers, both academic and trade, have created a new genre of book titles that confidently find the digital sizzle in the analog past: for example, *The Renaissance Computer* (on printed books), *The Victorian Internet* (on the telegraph), and *Social Media: The First 2,000 Years* (on letters, pamphlets, and graffiti). Scholars give talks with titles like "Books as Social Media" (Leah Price), "Blogging Now and Then (250 Years Ago)" (Robert Darnton), and "What's in a Visitor's Book? Social Media and Volcanic Tourism in the Nineteenth Century" (John Brewer).[3]

There is no doubt that we feel ourselves to be in the midst of a period of dramatic change in our media and information environments. My interest in this essay, however, lies not in these environments themselves, but rather in our popular uses of historical metaphor to explain them. Specifically, my interest lies in the practical and theoretical functions that historical metaphor serves in the intellectual marketplace. It is as common today for us to use the printing press as the central unit of measure in estimations of information history as it is for us to discuss our current circumstances in terms of an "information revolution." Surrounded as we are by these analogies – by these claims in favour of specific ways of construing the relationship between the past and the present, and by the significance claims that go with them – it seems fair to ask what purposes they serve. Situating an examination of this rhetoric within a larger discussion of the market forces that affect rhetorical practice, I seek to take a step in the direction of delimiting a context for the emergence of a distinctive set of contemporary tropes. What do these kinds of historical analogies mean for the ways in which we as futurists make use of history, and what do they mean for the ways in which we as historians take the long view? Why, in particular, do we turn to the rise of the printing press as our standard analogy for the rise of the Internet? What meanings does this metaphor constrain, what values does it offer to overwhelm those constraints, and what value does metaphoric thinking in general hold for analysis in media studies?

As this chapter shows, this rhetoric offers a powerful reminder of the extent to which technological discourse – inside as well as outside the academy – is obliged to respond to market imperatives. The tropes that join Zuckerberg with Gutenberg sell; thus they feature in the titles, cover blurbs, journalistic ledes, and other peripheral elements of texts that do not always advance the arguments they imply. Objections to the revolutionary myths of technological history – for example, that digital practice has failed to supplant the paper world or that computers possess no single or unified history – risk retreating from figure to ground when these elements are in play. Indeed, this set of tropes participates in a longer history of technological rhetoric that utilizes slippery language to shape the story of technological change in a form with popular appeal, a rhetoric that, as Leo Marx has noted, includes our uses of the word "technology" itself.

The analogy that joins "our time" with that of Johann Gutenberg, who invented the movable-type printing press in the mid-fifteenth century, precedes the Internet age, reaching back at least to the works of Marshall McLuhan in the 1960s and 1970s (especially his 1962 blockbuster, *The Gutenberg Galaxy*) and Walter Ong in the 1980s. McLuhan and Ong heralded an electronic age that seemed poised to return society, albeit somewhat differently configured, to the forms of orality that predated the era of print. For them, a medium was not only a vehicle of expression; it was an almost inevitable logic that could shape entire social constellations and forms of being. For example, while the logics that govern print culture include fixity, systematization, and multiplicity, oral culture – both in its "primary" (pre-print) and "secondary" (post-print) configurations – operates by logics of fluidity, instability, and collective composition.[4]

In 2007, the Danish scholar Lars Ole Sauerberg gave new life to this view of media history by introducing the concept of a "Gutenberg Parenthesis," a historical model that Thomas Pettit has done much to popularize.[5] This model frames the "culture of print" that came in the wake of the printing press as a temporary interlude rather than a permanent structural change: "a mere parenthesis between the oral world of almost all of history prior to the invention of the printing press and the secondary orality that we are experiencing as from the invention of the Internet."[6] The Gutenberg Parenthesis model seeks to unseat print culture from the throne of modernity and progress, suggesting instead that print culture, despite its apparent triumph over history, is in fact a temporary anomaly, with the prevailing order of human communication remaining on the side of speech and immediacy.[7]

For scholars working within a modern liberal framework, the appeal of this model is multidimensional. For one, the figure of the Gutenberg Parenthesis represents an effort to make media history less triumphalist. From the perspective of cultural pluralism, a valuable function of this historical model is that it presents the historical development of technology as an uneven pattern of recursion, restoration, and repetition, and thus allows the subject of literacy and orality to be pursued in the era of the Internet without reducing it to an argument about the civilized and the noncivilized. The printing press stands as the pivotal point that represents the beginning of the Gutenberg Parenthesis, just as the computer stands as the pivotal point that represents its end.

A second function of the model is to naturalize and effectively modernize the art of pre-modern eras, whether to make new authority claims as readers of old literature or to claim for ourselves, living in a time of tweets, viral videos, and other seemingly cheap and forgettable media forms, the power, grandeur, and rootedness of Shakespeare. Pettit portrays the Gutenberg Parenthesis as a framework with which we can connect "postmodern ideologies regarding artistic originality and appropriation" with the ideologies that governed Elizabethan aesthetic culture. By these lights, only the recent past is a foreign country; Shakespeare is revealed to have been a sophisticated practitioner of remix culture and a connoisseur of the database.[8] Thus a better understanding of our own culture prepares us to understand the attitudes and mores of the more distant past.[9] Writes a proponent of this view:

> In the context of this occasion and the cultural climate it
> breathes, the playmaking system of the Renaissance assumes a
> modernity – more precisely, a postmodernity – through the
> similarity of the modes of creative production before and after
> the parenthesis. Recognizing a "Gutenberg Parenthesis" makes
> it easier to recognize a theatre technology that overlapped with
> the print culture of the era Marshall McLuhan called the
> "Gutenberg Galaxy," which fifty years ago was not yet estab-
> lished in the critical vocabulary as a perception of a major par-
> adigm shift, much less of a passing phase. Shakespeare strad-
> dled the threshold, entering the parenthesis simultaneously
> with the actors of the commedia, whose literary progenitors
> were already in it, at least insofar as their plays were written in
> the hope of printing ... unstable cobbled pre-parenthetical the-
> ater that were excised when the texts were editorially stabilized
> for the press.[10]

Finally, the figure of the Gutenberg Parenthesis provides a model that allows scholars to theorize about media history in terms of stasis and disruption. For example, Jill Walker Rettberg, in an article that refers back to Pettit, claims that a look backward from the rise of print and print literacy can show us the same primordial soup that produced digital social media. We should celebrate, she says, that we have left the stiff and formal interim "dominated by print and its attendant norms such as the idea that you can have an autonomous, fixed text, or the idea that a text or cultural object is originally composed once, and thereafter passively reproduced by readers, musicians or performers."[11] Recently, Pettit has even proposed the historical existence of a "Privacy Parenthesis": a great pause between the semi-public life of the villager and the semi-public life of the netizen, during which culturally contingent values such as privacy and exclusivity came to seem like natural social rights.[12]

However, it is revealing that nearly all of these efforts to find the future in the past focus far less on understanding the past than on understanding the future. The use of popular terms like "social media" when discussing eighteenth- and nineteenth-century visitors' albums and commonplace books promises that we can identify the seeds of the future in the present by discovering our doppelgängers on the other side of a brief swerve in history. In both academic literature and the trade press, it has been a popular argument in recent years that the apparent endings we are witnessing in our own time – the end of privacy, the end of mass media, the end of the book – represent simply a return to the past, to a historical norm of greater stability and longer duration. The end of the printed book means the close of a Gutenberg parenthesis between manuscript networks and e-mail networks; the end of privacy is the close of a privacy parenthesis between the intrusiveness of the village well and the casual intrusiveness of Facebook stalking; the end of mass media is simply the end of a brief interlude in the nineteenth and twentieth centuries, supported by the economics of advanced industrial society, in which gathering and disseminating high-quality news was an easier and cheaper task for huge enterprises than for lay citizens.[13] Yet past and present have never joined up quite so easily. There is something admirable in the parenthesis approach to modelling history and its presentation of an alternative to the literature of elegy and nostalgia that has accompanied the "rise" of the digital age; yet the parenthesis approach itself succumbs to a false nostalgia (and a false parallelism) in the suggestion that a return to the past can heal a division that would otherwise be a wound. Any return to ways of being that can be identified as "past" must be a return with a substantial difference. Surely a lack of privacy in the village or the clan, when intimacy was intimacy with several hundred people, was a significantly different experience from a lack of privacy in a networked world of 7.4 billion people. As this book has set out to emphasize, the behaviour and configuration of audiences in digital spaces can differ significantly from those of their predecessors in other media systems; these differences affect the forms, dissemination, and uses of digital objects in ways that go beyond their formal essences.

2

Lars Ole Sauerberg, Pettit et al. do not hide the fact that their claims rely on associating specific periods of media technology with an intrinsic logic and trajectory. Part of my argument is that this association often implicitly attends more casual uses of the printing press metaphor, even when it is not explicitly stated. For this reason, I would like to pause briefly to discuss the recent history of this idea in media studies. Historians now tend to shy from the idea that technology is an entity capable of acting under an autonomous and self-derived logic (of course this remains a prevailing historical model for writers of popular nonfiction on technology and media). Raymond Williams, Adrian Johns, Michael Warner, and others have presented alternatives to views of media change in terms of internal logic or seismic rupture. These scholars argue that media change is gradual, iterative, and occurs in reciprocal exchange with change in other aspects of society.

Williams most famously articulates this view in his 1975 book, *Television: Technology and Cultural Form*, which argues that in the early years of any new medium – television included – that medium can move in any number of directions; in time, it settles down in a single direction, which then comes to seem natural and inevitable. Early witnesses of the rise of television failed to perceive many of the directions it might have taken, including a superior visual picture, in part because its definition as a "mass communication" medium obscured them. In the meanwhile, users of domestic television sets settled for an inferior standard of visual quality because of the social system that surrounded television broadcasting. "There were, in the abstract, several different ways in which television as a technical means might have been developed," Williams writes. "After a generation of universal domestic television it is not easy to realize this. But it remains true that, after a great deal of intensive research and development, the domestic television set is in a number of ways an inefficient medium of visual broadcasting."[14] Or, to borrow a phrase from evolutionary biology: not all traits are adaptations.

Johns turns a perspective informed, in part, by Williams to an analysis of the medium of print during its initial spread through European culture. Against the more deterministic claims of Marshall McLuhan, Elizabeth Eisenstein, and Alvin Kernan, among others – that the print medium enforced on the world of letters new logics of fixity, systematization, and the organization of information, in the process setting in motion the social and intellectual revolutions of the early modern period – he shows that it was necessary for human agents in the world of letters to enforce those qualities on printed texts.[15] The emergence of "stable," "reliable" editions of printed texts represented not fulfillments of an inherent print "logic," but rather the struggle of various literary and scientific communities to tame the messy and unstable world of print. Warner, meanwhile, works from the position that terms such as "new" media and "obsolete" technology act rather in the way the misleading term "mass communication" did (if Williams is right) in the early years of television, obscuring a more plural and pregnant reality. For Warner, this includes the reality that differing media systems always coexist – few ever become truly obsolete, and they all constantly renew themselves in response to one another.[16]

But the uses of tropes are a different matter from their accuracy. In practice these analogies draw upon their ability to tacitly present technology as an autonomous force that operates according to its own logic and in dramatic leaps. That media change occurs in seismic shifts, or that it occurs due to the autonomous "logic" of new technologies, are not widely held ideas in media studies, but nonetheless they form the core of some of the most widely used narratives in media studies. In this view, the printing press is a ubiquitous analogy for the computer in part because it readily summons narratives of seismic innovation. As I will discuss, the popularity of these metaphors may best be attributed to marketplace pressures in Silicon Valley and the academic marketplace of ideas. While we normally imagine debate in terms of challengers vying for dominance in the marketplace, there are times when the presence of a marketplace itself acts as a dominating force, and this is true, albeit in different ways, in industry and the university alike.

This pattern places the printing press metaphor in a lineage of technological rhetoric that includes the terms *information* and even *technology* itself. The philosopher Leo Marx has argued that over the course of the twentieth century, the term technology became a misleading and philosophically "hazardous" concept, used largely as a placeholder to fill a void between the artifacts we create and the kinds of social change we want to discuss. As I discuss below, the role – one of the roles – that the printing press metaphor serves in the discourse of technological change resembles the role that Marx has identified for the concept of "technology." The effort to find the key term or analogy to label our own time belongs to a predictive impulse: an assumption, often buried but still forceful, that technological culture develops according to an autonomous force and essence, and that by identifying this essence we can gain a privileged vantage point onto the future.

In our general uses of it, the printing press as a symbol of technological change likewise tends to imply that historical change is revolutionary and progressive. Marx connects projections of this kind with the uses we make of the term "technology." The term is particularly dangerous, Marx says, when we use it in ways that attribute to "technology" autonomy and agency, as in "Technology is changing the way we live."[17] The word in its current sense is in fact a recent coinage. Up through the late nineteenth century, "the word *technology* primarily referred to a kind of book; except for a few lexical pioneers, it was not until the turn of this century that sophisticated writers like Thorstein Veblen began to use the word to mean the mechanic arts collectively. But that sense of the word did not gain wide currency until after World War I."[18] The OED records early uses of the term "technology" to refer to "a discourse or treatise on an art or arts." In 1615, for example, Sir George Buck's *Third University of England*, a "report of the sciences, arts, and faculties" in the city of London, speaks of "an apt close of this general Technologie." In 1706, *Phillip's New World of Words* defines "technology" as "a Description of Arts, especially the Mechanical." As late as 1860, the magazine *Vanity Fair*, waggishly proposing a new "Dictionary for Congressmen," was able to include "technologies" in the flood of dictionaries that characterized the age: "We have Classical Dictionaries, Dictionaries of Science, Dictionaries of Art, Rhyming Dictionaries, – by which those who are not born Poets may achieve Poetry, or, rather, have Poetry thrust upon them, – Cyclopædias and Technologies without Number."[19]

Rather in the way that, according to Williams, the pressures of technological innovation respond to prevailing ideologies and new social needs, the word technology rose to dominance in our discourse by adapting to the needs of the moment. It better served an emerging system of belief about history and progress than prior terms for the same general concept, such as *the mechanic arts, the practical arts*, and *the industrial arts*. This system of belief included, first, the joining of an earlier Enlightenment belief in historical progress (i.e., a view of history as a force moving toward more advanced and enlightened stages of civilization) with a newer belief that both scientific and mechanical innovation were responsible for, and indeed constituted, this movement. The Enlightenment conception of history, as Kant articulated it, assumed first that history has a forward impulse and a destination, and second, that this destination consists of political progress, which improvements in the mechanical arts might help (but only help) to bring about. In the early nineteenth century, people began to speak as though improvements in the mechanical arts were themselves the goal toward which history moves, and thus constitute what people continued to call "progress." This conceptual shift entailed a new treatment of history as the story of man's intellectual conquest of nature. Together, Marx argues, these ideological changes "created a semantic void, that is, a set of social circumstances for which no adequate concept was yet available – a void that the new concept, *technology*, eventually would fill."[20]

A factor that sharpened the urgency of this "conceptual void" was the specific form that the most visible improvements in the mechanic arts took during the Industrial Revolution. The railway, the

electric telegraph, and other defining features of industrial life entailed massive and rhizomic social, bureaucratic, and mechanical
systems, difficult to separate and each a complex entity in its own
right. The railway alone required, besides the engine itself: "(1) various kinds of ancillary equipment (rolling stock, stations, yards,
bridges, tunnels, viaducts, signal systems, and a huge network of
tracks); (2) a corporate business organization with a large capital investment; (3) specialized forms of technical knowledge (railroad
engineering, telegraphy); (4) a specially trained work force with
unique railroading skills, including civil and locomotive engineers,
firemen, telegraphers, brakemen, conductors – a work force large
and resourceful enough to keep the system going day and night, in
all kinds of weather, 365 days a year; and (5) various facilitating institutional charges, such as laws establishing standardized track
gauges and a national system of standardized time zones."[21]

The shrinking (in systems like the railway) of the "pivotal arti-
factual component" in relation to the whole sharpened the need
for a term that could refer to a complex system while seeming to
refer to a specific instrument. Further, in keeping with the conceptual shift toward a sense that industrial change is a goal in its
own right, this semantic need entailed a meaning that would en-
compass not only an instrument in the service of progress, but also
the fact of progress itself.[22] The term technology emerged to fill
that need. Thus we can say today that automotive technology (for
example) permeates the world in the form of cars, trucks, roads
and highway infrastructure, the shipping and delivery industries,
industries for materials such as steel and glass, through to the
abstract benefits of living in an automotive society. Computer
technology is likewise omnipresent, from pads, phones, and PCs
through to children's toys, washing machines, sewage systems,
power plants, and, of course, automotive technology.[23] The value of
the term technology lies in its very ambiguity. As Marx writes, in
reference to the concept of "the machine": "The whole issue becomes irrelevant once we recognize that we are dealing with a
metaphor, and that its immense appeal rests, not on its capacity to
describe the actual character of industrialization, but rather on its
vivid suggestiveness. It evokes the uniqueness of a new way of life,

as experienced, and, most important, it is a vivid expression of the affinity between technology and the great political revolution of modern times."[24]

Like the railway engine – or the computer chip – the printing press is a small material artifact that readily elides into a much larger social, organizational, and mechanical system, the scope of which is vast and indeterminate. The view of the effects of the printing press that Walter Ong promoted (that the transition from "oral culture" to "literate culture," along with the changes this implies in terms of education, cultural production, trade, and so forth, was immediate and thoroughgoing) and the opposing position that eventually succeeded him (that these changes were slow and gradual) both participate in the post-industrial rhetoric that elides a single artifact with an unknowably large system. In short, the metaphor of the printing press serves in our discourse much the same role that Marx has identified for the concept of technology. The trope is useful precisely because our understanding of its boundaries is so nebulous that we can apply the trope without having to commit to any specific point of reference.

Indeed, building on Marx's lead, Paul Duguid has recently argued that information is a term that takes on a problematic anachronism when we use it in reference to periods before the quite recent past. In a lecture at Harvard in 2014, he stressed the changes in meaning that the term has undergone throughout the history of its usage. Until the mid-nineteenth century, the word information was a transferred use of the verb to inform, rather in the way that delineation is a transferred use of the verb to delineate. For much of the twentieth century, the term vacillated between vague meanings in popular usage and quite different specific meanings in specialist terminology. For example Claude Shannon, the father of information theory, separated *information* from *meaning*, a distinction that runs counter to common usage. Duguid argues persuasively that we have come more recently to use the word information as a placeholder, a catchall term for phenomena we don't know how to identify or describe.[25]

In short, when we use the printing press as a metaphor for changes in our information culture, we succumb to anachronism twice. First, this metaphorical use relies on a now-belated concept, dating to the aftermath of the Industrial Revolution, of a single artifact that can represent a wider matrix of political, social, cultural, and institutional effects while diffusing specific claims about what those effects might be. Our understanding of the effects of the printing press is so multifarious that we can, and generally do, apply the figure as a placeholder for the unknown. By comparing changes in our information culture to changes that the printing press "created" in an earlier information culture, we open our claim to include a wide range of possible meanings, but in the process we drain the comparison of specific value. Second, and more importantly, by unreflectively using the printing press as a metaphor for changes in an information culture, we elide long-term shifts in ideology and material practice that may represent the most important forms of difference among various media systems. The interface designs of social-media platforms often invite us to discuss those platforms using language and rubrics borrowed from older media, notably bibliographic history. These metaphors represent a useful and knowing anachronism insofar as their histories provide concepts that we employ as heuristics while using and navigating digital environments; still, they can obscure the changes in textual and social relations that are emerging around these digital heuristics. A complicated root system of genealogies connects digital textuality to cinematic, theatrical, bibliographic, and – to distinguish the codes of bibliography from social institutions of letters – literary modes of communication. We can also add the genealogy of games, a form of play that social-media platforms deliberately elicit in order to keep the reader perpetually engaged in the activities of reading, navigating, and adding to the body of the text.

### 3

Another context that illuminates the marketplace value of the printing press metaphor is that of Silicon Valley. The distinctive incentive structures of Silicon Valley – start-up culture, venture capital financing, payment in stock options, IPOs – are geared toward the rhetoric of revolutionary change. For a company seeking investors to claim that the near future will be radically changed from the present, and that this change will be predicated on the autonomous force of changing technologies, implies that the future is manageable and claims ownership of that terrain. It recommends investors to the company and consumers to its products. To claim that technological change is gradual, iterative, unpredictable, and never fully complete, and that the future of technology will depend at least as much on social and cultural factors as on machinery viewed in isolation, would obviously be a weaker sell.[26]

Yet industry practice can differ dramatically from the public narratives that technology companies present. The books on business strategy and innovation that have enjoyed the most success and influence within the technology sector often present, by contrast with public narratives of revolution and upheaval, a granular and iterative narrative of technological change. For example, Clayton Christensen's theory of disruptive innovation, most famously articulated in a best-selling 1997 book, *The Innovator's Dilemma*, proposes that technological change in the marketplace often occurs as lower-cost, lower-quality technologies gradually eat up the market share of higher-quality technologies.[27] Not only is Christensen's book (and his follow-up books on the same subject) an enduring best seller in industry, but also corporations such as Apple implement business strategies that put into practice the view of technological change he advocates; for example, creating smaller, semi-independent companies that are meant to gradually "disrupt" Apple's current products, at which point they will be absorbed back into the Apple mothership.[28]

In a 2003 article in the *Harvard Business Review*, Nicholas Carr directed attention toward the relationship between the incentive structures of the digital economy and the ways in which commentators embedded in those structures frame and direct historical comparison. These comparisons, he argues, tend to emphasize moments of revolutionary change, a structure that coheres with the hype-driven framework of venture capital financing: "Many commentators have drawn parallels between the expansion of IT, particularly the Internet, and the rollouts of earlier technologies. Most of the comparisons, though, have focused on either the investment pattern associated with the technologies – the boom-to-bust cycle – or the technologies' roles in reshaping the operations of entire industries or even economies. Little has been said about the way the technologies influence, or fail to influence, competition at the firm level."[29]

At stake in this form of historical comparison is an understanding of the actual role of computers in the contemporary business world, a role that Carr describes as distinctly non-revolutionary. Carr argues that once a new technology moves past the relatively short phase of being a "proprietary" technology – the phase during which only one or a few companies can benefit from the use of that technology – it becomes an "infrastructural" technology, which everyone uses and which therefore confers no comparative advantage. Technology firms that rely on venture capital funding and the sale of stock options therefore have a substantial incentive to behave as though they are perpetually in the proprietary cycle. Their rhetoric reflects this fact. But such rhetoric is highly misleading, he argues; most computing technologies become infrastructural technologies in a relatively short time.[30]

Another context is commercial publishing, the world's most ferocious attention economy. Incentive structures in publishing, too, reward rhetoric that frames computing technology in terms of revolutionary change. In the trade press, which is, after all, self-consciously a consumer market, this relationship is less troubled; books on technology abound whose titles include the word "revolution" or suggest its tenor. Examples include *The Soft Edge: A Natural History and Future of the Information Revolution, Groundswell: Winning in a World Transformed by Social Technologies*, and *Smarter than Us: The Rise of Machine Intelligence*.[31] Academic publishing, too, seems to manifest a perception that the market rewards depictions of media change as revolutionary and technology-driven, although this perception is in tension with prevailing academic theories of media change. Consider, for example, the stream of recent books on computing whose titles turn on the famous name of Gutenberg, among them *From Gutenberg to the Global Information Infrastructure* (2000), *From Gutenberg to Google* (2006), and *From*

*Gutenberg to Zuckerberg* (2011).[32] Some of these books argue that Gutenberg effectively restarted the calendar, initiating an epoch governed by a distinctive logic. Others do not, but for the sake of the market they still take advantage of the famous name.

That this phenomenon is most pronounced in the aspects of published works that are directly associated with the marketplace, such as titles, blurbs, and other framing devices, shows that these pressures affect the tactics even of authors who reject a seismic view of technological change. For example, in a widely praised media studies book of recent years, Asa Briggs and Peter Burke's *Social History of the Media: From Gutenberg to the Internet*, the authors take care to emphasize that the social history of media does not actually begin with Gutenberg, and that media change is a diffuse and nonlinear process: "This book concentrates on the modern west, from the late fifteenth century onwards. The narrative begins with printing (c. AD 1450) rather than with the alphabet (c. 2000 BC), with writing (c. 5000 BC), or with speech, but despite the importance often attributed to Johann Gutenberg (c. 1400–68), whom readers of one British newspaper voted 'man of the millennium' (*Sunday Times*, 28 November 1999), there is no clean break or zero point at which the story begins, and it will sometimes be necessary to refer briefly back to the ancient and medieval worlds."[33]

Yet the most visible parts of the book telescope our attention to those zero points of the press and the Internet: not only the title, but also the image on the cover, which places together, in a pas de deux, the letter "i" (a common symbol of Internet culture) and a printing press. This sort of motif is common. The cover illustration of *From Gutenberg to Zuckerberg* is a printing press that is visibly emitting a Wi-Fi signal.

Trade books, which sell solutions as much as they do analysis, may have a special incentive to claim that changes in media technologies create changes in human consciousness. Nicholas Carr's bestseller *The Shallows* opens with the claim that "For the last five centuries, ever since Gutenberg's printing press made book reading a popular pursuit, the linear, literary mind has been at the centre of art, science, and society."[34] But although critics such as Briggs and Burke have moved away from models like Carr's, which echoes McLuhan and Ong in its longing look back at a vanishing or vanished mentality, the framing elements in their works often tacitly endorse these models. In this sense, the marketplace exerts a strong enough force that scholars can find themselves making implicit claims in favour of views of media culture and media change that they question or even explicitly oppose. These claims serve functions that are valuable enough in the attention economy of ideas that we may find ourselves deploying them, however unwillingly, against our own arguments.

Indeed, framing the computer narrowly as a communications instrument makes it more available to academic discourse considered as a marketplace. It is reasonable to acknowledge that communication has played a large role in the history of computing; digital computers rely on symbol processing, for example, and the most high-profile functions of modern computers involve communication.[35] Yet it is also reasonable to acknowledge that the history of computers includes many genealogies besides the one that runs through the history of communication.[36] From the perspective of humanities discourse, the most obvious benefit of framing the computer as a communications instrument to the exclusion of all else is that it translates all that computers produce into communication. If everything is discourse, then everything can be analyzed discursively. In critical discourse, the printing press metaphor enables us to evoke a sense of forward movement and developmental logic that enhances the significance and narrative coherence of the histories we tell. We can also see elements of such an agenda in the buried metaphors that pervade narratives of media and literary history, such as the "rise" of print and the "rise" of the book. In short, although neither the academy nor Silicon Valley think of the computer as only a communications instrument, both recognize benefits in linking computers to a communications-based genealogy. Even when they acknowledge the diversity of the forms and functions of computing technology, media theorists often find themselves obliged to narrow those functions for the sake of a narrative they can claim as their own.

A famous and effective theorist of this form of self-contradiction is Pierre Bourdieu. I invoke him in this chapter simply in order to indicate that the problem is not new, even if it is distinctively of our own time. He describes its operations in several places, but especially in the essay "Flaubert and the French Literary Field," where he classifies cultural producers and intellectuals under the description "dominated dominants."[37] As producers of ideology, these figures hold positions of dominance within a culture's general field of power; but they are themselves dominated by the need for success within a marketplace, and in that sense they resemble – if perhaps are not one with – the dominated.[38] Bourdieu writes of the conditions that produce these figures:

> The literary and artistic field is contained within the field of power, while possessing a relative autonomy with respect to it, especially as regards its economic and political principles of hierarchization. It occupies a dominated position (at the negative pole) in this field, which is itself situated at the dominant pole of the field of class relations. It is thus the site of a double hierarchy: the heteronomous principle of hierarchization, which would reign unchallenged if, losing all autonomy, the literary and artistic field were to disappear as such (so that writers and artists became subject to the ordinary laws prevailing in the field of power, and more generally in the economic field), is success, as measured by indices such as book sales, number of theatrical performances, etc., or honors, appointments, etc.[39]

In Bourdieu's analysis, in a capitalist society, those who hold economic capital enjoy positions of dominance in the field of power, while those who hold cultural capital find themselves in an ambiguous position of gilded subordination: they help to articulate the values and ideas of their time, and they often find themselves under pressure to legitimate existing power structures, but they can also criticize those structures and disseminate subversive views. The scholars and critics who discuss technology in the marketplace of ideas, as well as the tech companies that seek to stand out in the crowded attention economy of Silicon Valley, represent distinctively twenty-first-century versions of this concept. While in theory and indeed in practice they subscribe to the idea that technological change is gradual and iterative, they regularly invoke the spirit of revolutionary technology because it attracts attention and creates valuable claims for the authority and significance of their work. Although they hold a dominant position in the culture, they are dominated by the marketplace, which is the true form of power.

4

Van Dijck identifies the rise of social media with the kinds of revolutionary narrative that I have just discussed. During the first decade of the twenty-first century, as social-media platforms decisively took the fore as major publishers, new commercial narratives arose; with Lessig, media theorists celebrated new, "hybrid" models of amateur peer production set within commercial frameworks. Gradually, however, the assumptions that supported these platforms "divulged a new set of norms and values staked in the ideology of technological progress and neoliberalism."[40] The doctrine of technological progress, in particular, naturalizes the expansion of connective media and of a few platforms in particular. "Platform tactics such as the popularity principle and ranking mechanisms hardly involve contingent technological structures; instead, they are firmly rooted in an ideology that values hierarchy, competition, and a winner-takes-all mind-set." Specific values and keywords of the culture of connective media – networking, sharing, oversharing, information wants to be free – benefit the platform owners by creating momentum for the growth of the connective media ecosystem.[41]

Discussions of dominant "symbolic forms" in the digital age have often focused on the so-called "dyad" of narrative and database. The origin of this discourse is Lev Manovich's classic work, *The Language of New Media*, where Manovich describes database and narrative as opponents, with database superseding narrative, in the digital age, as the dominant cultural form.[42] He writes: "As a cultural form, database represents the world as a list of items and it refuses to order this list. In contrast, a narrative creates a cause-and-effect trajectory of seemingly unordered items (events). Therefore, database and narrative are natural enemies. Competing for the same territory of human culture, each claims an exclusive right to make meaning out of the world."[43]

Responding to Manovich, N. Katherine Hayles – while supporting the claim that database and narrative are "different species" – has persuasively argued that they act not as enemies, but as symbionts.[44] The unordered structure of database gives us new tools for finding patterns in masses of information, but after we have done the work of finding patterns, we use narrative to give those patterns meaningful forms, such as argument or cause and effect. Moreover, we use the narratives (which includes the implicit hierarchies) of our disciplines in order to determine how to generate, collect, and categorize the data in our databases. In Lisa Gitelman's memorable phrase, "raw data is an oxymoron."[45]

Other critics have tended to redraw this dyad while moving to resolve its tension. A 2007 special issue of PMLA is a case in point. There, Jerome McGann argues that a scholarly resource that we might regard as a database is not really the unordered entity that Manovich describes. Instead, its significant features will emerge from its user interface, which (along with the markup languages that support the interface) represents a form of organization if not narrative, and thus gives the lie to the claim that the data being managed is unorganized.[46] Ed Folsom goes further, suggesting that a database can actualize the metaphor of an archive via design elements in the user interface. The *Walt Whitman Archive* (the subject of the special issue) is a database in a literal sense, as a digital structure that stores data; but it is also an archive in a metaphorical sense, "meant to evoke the dust and texture and smell of the old books and documents themselves."[47] The user interface gives this metaphor the force of substantiality.

The continuing triumph of the desktop interface should remind us of the importance of metaphors as heuristic guides for understanding new media systems. As Jay David Bolter has remarked, the desktop metaphor is misleading because it renders computerized labour as virtual and effortless.[48] It is also misleading because it conjures a paper-based world that computers aim to render obsolete. Concepts of the digital "page" *as* a page – whether for a Word document, a "notebook" application, or a webpage – likewise exist in tension with the precursor they mean to supplant. Interface metaphors that connect online publishing systems to concepts and practices from bibliographic history – author, chapter, page, book-mark – help users to cope with alterity. However, it may disguise the extent to which the practices that take place under these signi-fiers have diverged from bibliographic tradition. In this book, I have argued that the much-discussed tension between the opera-tions of the digital environment, on the one hand, and narratives and metaphors belonging to print culture, on the other, is useful-ly complicated by attention to game mechanics. Van Dijck stresses that technologies affect our social values and social configurations: "Sociality is not simply 'rendered technological' by moving to an online space; rather, coded structures are profoundly altering the nature of our connections, creations, and interactions."[49] In what follows, I will examine the tension between the narratives that in-form the interface level of these platforms and the social practices that arise from their game mechanics.

In his classic book on design theory, *The Design of Everyday Things*, Donald Norman emphasizes the role of "mental models" in enabling users to understand how systems function.[50] Designing the interface (what Norman calls the system image) to cohere with existing mental models (or "the models people have of themselves, others, the environment, and the things with which they interact") helps users to operate systems without instruction.[51] But interface metaphors are not merely figures in space; as Norman explains, mental models, as explanatory devices, both result from and pro-duce narratives that develop over time.[52] With this in mind, we might regard the bibliographic metaphors that inform, at the level of interface, the new publishing platforms of social media to par-ticipate in narratives of technological progress that give the new platforms an aura of inevitability. The library of the past must de-velop into the virtual library of the future; this shift is inevitable, a sign of technology unfolding as it should. Certainly, critics have often discussed YouTube, Facebook, and AO3, for example, in the terms of an archive or a library, responding to cues in their design that figure these platforms in terms of known cultural institutions.[53] For example, critics have debated whether we should regard YouTube as an archive, since many of the clips it makes available "present, and thus make accessible, historic material," or rather as a library, which, like YouTube, is meant for reference but not necessarily for storage, and which deals with copies but not originals.[54] However, both of these functional metaphors fail to adequately describe the platform. YouTube takes no interest, as archives do, in permanent storage, and it lacks the specific "rules and regulations" that define libraries as an institution.[55]

Facebook has been among the most successful platforms to transform a skeuomorphic design into a narrative of technological inevitability. It is well known that the site began as an online spin on an existing institution, the paper "facebook" that universities distributed to undergraduates.[56] An early goal of the site was to appear as a natural technological progression of student identity. In a 2006 interview, one of Facebook's founders commented that the company was trying to make joining Facebook seem unavoidable: "If you don't have a Facebook profile, you don't have an online identity." Ryan Bigge criticizes this "narrative of inevitability" as a false narrative that aims to lure in users and push them to produce regular content, with the alternative of non-existence. The success of this strategy can be measured not only in the massive user base the site now enjoys, but also in the large-scale narratives that we now deploy to situate modern identity in a historical context leading from analog publics to social-media publics.[57] Countless op-eds, thinkpieces, and academic papers have extended narratives that, by construing our lives as social-media lives, place us on the far side of a wave of historical change. This discourse persisted as Facebook shifted its interface design away from an imitation of paper facebooks and toward the suite of features that this book has discussed. But as Bigge reminds us, it continued to rely on narratives in which old technological regimes inexorably unfold into new ones.[58] Bigge also remarks, quoting another media scholar, on the prominent spectre in these narratives of the autonomous force of technology: "Modern (and now postmodern) technology is routinely understood as an autonomous, disembodied force operating behind any specific application, the effect of a system that is somehow much less material, more ubiquitous, than any mere 'machinery.'"[59]

From this perspective, activity on Facebook might seem to present another instance of the modern synergy between narrative and database. On the one hand, activity on Facebook both produces and is circumscribed by narratives: the narratives of selfhood that social media fosters, which scholars such as dana boyd have incisively described, and larger narratives of dramatic technological change.[60] On the other hand, the content that results from activity on Facebook – texts, music, videos, images, forms of user-produced feedback such as likes, as well as hidden layers of metadata about browsing habits – is stored and made available via database structures. "All this personal information, plus a user's activities, are stored in essentially a huge database, where it can be analyzed, manipulated, systematized, formalized, classified and aggregated." Critics have often deplored the "oversharing" that takes place on social media as a cultural flaw rather than a guided result. Yet, as we have seen, social-media platforms encourage continuous user activity as a matter of design. One of Bigge's interview subjects griped that Facebook's settings "always assumed you wanted to share more rather than less" – a complaint that fits entirely with a view of social-media platforms as publishers that are explicitly structured by the need to elicit steady content.[61] So crucial is the constant flow of content to social-media platforms, and the management of this deluge by database systems, that Geert Lovink has described the rise of such platforms as "the database turn."[62]

Media scholars have sought to identify a distinctive aesthetics for database-anchored platforms. For instance, Lovink says of YouTube, "We no longer watch films or TV; we watch databases."[63] By this, Lovink means two things. First, we have abandoned our reliance on traditional arbiters of taste; algorithms and linked entities now guide what we watch, rather than reviewers and theatre owners. Second, "YouTubing" places activity itself – the active present tense of browsing, searching, clicking – at the fore: "The hunt for (and among) moving images is becoming just as important as looking at the search results. But we're all too happy to integrate

YouTube into our busy daily lives so we don't have to think about the implications of watching the computer 24/7. It's already a cultural fact that we take TV everywhere with us and watch a quick clip while we're waiting at the bus stop. What does it mean that our attention is being guided by database systems? Is searching really more important than finding?"[64]

The first chapter of this book suggested that continual activity is an essential condition of online textuality. In its attention to broadcast over storage, both at the level of coded features and at the level of user experience, YouTube fits this specification. It is true that YouTube deals in videos, not texts – excluding the comment section – but it belongs to the ecosystem of connective media that this book has been examining; it interacts with other such platforms via embedded share buttons, and like them, it is a social-media platform that has a database system as its technological basis. It is notable, therefore, that media scholars who discuss YouTube's database aesthetics – Lovink is one; F. Kessler and M.T. Schaefer are others – describe YouTube as a database in strict technological terms, but in the terms of subjective experience, emphasize the sense of living activity over Manovich's database aesthetics of "unordered items."[65] Write Kessler and Schaefer, "YouTubing in many ways goes beyond the activity of merely watching videos … The interface offers many possibilities for users to participate: starting a channel, uploading videos, adding titles, tags, and comments, liking, sharing."[66] Our felt experience of the platform pulls against what conventional database aesthetics should emphasize, namely matters of hierarchy and organization.[67] This is not accidental, for the database back end of YouTube exists to manage precisely the kinds of information that arise from perpetual flows of user production and consumption. The content that users generate includes not only channels and video files, but also comments, likes, shares, and follows; metadata such as flags for inappropriate content; and user activity data, "such as the number of views, popularity ratings, and recursive links."[68] All of this information, not merely video files, makes up the content of YouTube's database system. From front to back end, the platform is designed to support active play, reflecting what Stuart Moulthrop describes as a wider "shift from narrative

to ludic engagement with texts and from interpretation to configuration."[69] Moreover, because of YouTube's integration into the
connective media ecosystem writ large, the bounded, competitive
play of YouTubing continues on other platforms, as well.[70]

I would like to suggest that we think of activity in the textual
ecosystem of social media in terms of a set of organizing structures
that include not only narrative and database, but also game. Databases store and retrieve content; narrative is embedded in the
metaphors that make an interface usable, and arises as companies,
critics, and individual users build meaning from the content. But another paradigmatic form that affects the shapes that the content may
take and the patterns of activity with which users engage with content is *game*; in this form, users break content – what would be "unordered items" for a database and a "cause-and-effect trajectory" for
a narrative – into items to be exchanged within rule-bound, interactive configurations, the rules for which are provisional and subject
to constant mutation.[71] Game is not narrative, as Juul and others
have extensively shown; but game and narrative, in constituting, together, the front-end experience of connective media, maintain a relationship that is not so much oppositional as synergistic.

As Janet Murray has discussed, game scholars already recognize
a certain synergy between game and narrative. This was apparent
even in the so-called "debate" between ludology (the study of
games from the perspective of abstract rules) and narratology (in
this context, the study of games from the perspective of narrative),
which always entailed more synergy than opposition.[72] Rebellion
against narrative served for some game scholars as a useful posture,
producing a negative space against which they could better define
the terms of games as a distinctive aesthetic form; but few suggested that narratives are absent in games or the study of narratives irrelevant to them. As Espen Aarseth commented, "The real irony of
the 'ludology vs narratology' 'debate' is that virtually all the so-
called ludologists are actually trained in narratology."[73] "In fact,"
writes Murray, "no one has been interested in making the argument that there is no difference between games and stories or that
games are merely a subset of stories. Those interested in both
games and stories see game elements in stories and story elements

in games: interpenetrating sibling categories, neither of which completely subsumes the other."[74]

According to this view, the study of content production on these sites must take into account phenomena separate from narrative meaning-making and interpretation. A recognition of the narrative elements that inform the interface design of social-media platforms (and, relatedly, surround their public narratives of technological emergence) can help us to understand how users derive meaning from their activity. But attention to the ludic, "configurational" properties of user activity can help us to better understand user behaviour writ large.[75] These ludic properties stand outside of the grand narratives that define connective media in terms of a line of descent from literary media and ultimately the revolution of the printing press; as such, they are easily overlooked or subsumed into a literary history that has always included minor subcultures that based creativity on rule-bound play. As this book has argued, however, the dominance of game mechanics over the publishing landscape of connective media represents a change in both scale and scope. If, with Manovich, we choose to regard the database as a paradigmatic structure of Web 1.0, then perhaps we can view the game as a paradigm of Web 2.0, with its demand for steady user activity disguised as play.[76] Database, narrative, game: a triad of synergistic organizing structures that define, at present, the culture of social media.

# 5

## Epilogue

Textual culture on the publishing platforms of social media has quietly undergone a sea change, drawing its momentum from the pleasures of keeping an infinite game in play. This book has argued that the change has its basis not only in the formal properties of the medium but also in the social dynamics of the audience, which has shifted from interpreting the objects of its attention to endlessly reworking them (configuration), and the functional parameters of the text, which include structures of rapid feedback and voluntary constraint. In the epilogue, I revisit major themes from the preceding chapters and consider one further challenge for literary scholars in the new world of letters. Artifacts have politics, as Langdon Winner famously argued.[1] Increasingly, the media forms that manage and transmit the materials of the humanities are the creations of designers and engineers who adhere to disciplinary philosophies quite different from what traditional humanistic training confers; for this reason, in order to understand the values and concerns that shape new media, we need to attend to the distinctive ways in which the people who produce new media come together. While individual scholars have already done heroic work in this direction, a conspicuous divide persists between the cultures of these communities and the methods of graduate training in the humanities. Widening our cultural contacts will help us to incorporate new genealogies into our understanding of the history of new media.

# 1

*Vale atque ave*: there is no better way to learn about something than to bid farewell to it. In our own time, the instance of this general truth that feels most distinctive, at least from a perspective within the humanities, is a wide sense of defamiliarization with "the book" as we knew it. Publishers seek, with limited success thus far, to discover the future of books by designing e-books that feature interactive reading experiences, multimedia storytelling, and formal excitements such as hyperlinks. Literary scholars are using the existence of new media as an impetus to reconsider the narratives and categories that we use to make sense of the literary system. Notably, scholars are also showing a greater readiness to part with the idea of literature as a category defining something essential and stable.[2] And yet – inevitably – the handles that we use to make sense of the new media forms retain the imprints of older media, if only as a matter of skeuomorphic design. In the university, in the publishing business, in the new textual ecosystems of the Web, our conversations about the digital future of texts continue to revolve, in important ways, around the memory of books, archives, and libraries.

Beneath and around these reminiscences, the public is encountering still other social and institutional changes. The production and circulation of texts in the digital environment – including, but not limited to, the five major categories of online discourse: fiction, news, analysis, gossip, and humblebragging – reflects the circumstance that many widely used online publishing platforms, which account for the new epistolary networks of social media, an increasing share of the news market, and a massive amount of fiction being written and published today, rely for their cultural identities – even, to an extent, for their existence – on game mechanics. Newshounds use Twitter to link and comment on stories from newspapers all over the world. Teenagers hang out on pseudonymous social networks, extending the terms of the group interaction by sharing, and responding to, new sets of instructions for playing: here is a picture: produce another that riffs on the same theme; here is a hashtag: produce content that fits it; here is a numbered list of questions: send me a number, and I will answer the corresponding question. Readers of book series gather in forums to discuss characters, exchange theories, and show off their own drawings, videos, and musical compositions based on the source material. Newspaper journalists – old media conceding to new – devise stories and headlines with an eye to garnering likes, links, and shares on social media, also known as *social media optimization*. All of this activity occurs, on these platforms, within point systems that rank the performances, direct attention to popular content, and motivate new production. These point systems, as well as the higher-order games of changing patterns of constraint that users have built above them, reflect a distinctive feature of these publishing platforms: they are designed to encourage users to generate content as a leisure activity. Game scholars like Ian Bogost may not like the corporate practice of gamification – their epithet pointsification is apt, if beside the point – but from a standpoint that is descriptivist, rather than prescriptivist, these mechanics *exist* regardless of whether we like them, and they exist because they are seen to have an effect.

The idea that textual production in any major literary system might share a direct lineage with games has not previously been part of the self-understanding of the humanities. As I wrote in the first chapter, the question of whether games are art is familiar to the point of tedium; the question of whether art is a game is less often asked and harder to answer. This book set out to examine the digital practice of imbricating game mechanics into other kinds of activities and the effects that these mechanics have had on specific textual communities. An obvious effect has been to drive up the production of texts, exacerbating the problem of "information overload" that, if it is not specific to our media environment, received a name because our media environment made it imperative to discuss, to diagnose as a symptom of the age. In tandem with this process, mechanics such as points have provided new forms of metadata for managing oceans of text, more folkish – more audience-oriented – than catalogue data in libraries. Texts that the audience has judged as winning performances are more likely to appear on your screen, via algorithms that tally points; texts that have been judged as truly winning appear on everyone's screens, having gone viral. The quest to *go viral*, or at least to win points, is a widely acknowledged motivator for user production. Information management shapes information production.

Another effect concerns the uses of genre, which exhibits – for example in fan fiction communities – a prolixity that seems related to its ability to confer productive constraint. Writing communities have always used genre as a form of productive constraint, but in no previous media ecosystem did writing communities observe such an abundance of genres and genre-like motifs; not only familiar literary genres, like romance, fantasy, and drama, but scores of hashtag prompts, holiday prompts, and vanishingly specific micro-genres define the ordinary culture of fan fiction. These genres play an active and formative role in shaping new production; they are occasions to produce, and writers use them as temporary terms for play. As prosumers, writers, too, follow a different suite of practices in the read-write environment than they did in the read-only environment of print.[3] And the reception of art of all kinds has taken on new dimensions in the hi-tech game economy: we circulate pieces of official media works to attract responses, like sucker fish, around them; fashion new art from old in the pursuit of viral glory; participate in real-time competitions of commentary; turn audience responses into genre-like motifs to imitate. In terms of live performance and interactive experience, these matrices of reception relate, structurally, to chess and card games, as they also relate to archives, libraries, and variorums. Such alternate genealogies may contribute new materials to our efforts to theorize reception and audiences in the network era.

However, the book has restricted its focus to the boundaries of the platforms themselves and the textual activity that takes place on them. There are other discussions – of aesthetic merit, of the larger cultural formations that shape digital technologies, of the relationship between the platform era and the surveillance era – that the subject matter of this book may gesture toward, but that ultimately still lie beyond its perimeters. For example, one scholar has argued of Tudor court poetry – based largely on its unoriginality, its extensive borrowing – that "the study of these poems belongs to sociology rather than to literature."[4] Should we adopt such a stance toward fan fiction, if we understand that activity in the terms of game play? Such a closing of the gates is distasteful from an ecumenical perspective, but then again the enduring frameworks of Romantic art – a stable text, a solitary author – have truly limited application in that culture. Or again, Christian Fuchs, among others, has examined the connection between surveillance and social media.[5] If we circulate news and commentary, the traditional meaning of the public sphere, on social media sites that not only use design features that encourage a maximal flow of information, but also collect further, privileged information about the activity of the participants themselves, how does this affect the model of the public sphere in the network era?[6]

To a lesser extent, this book considered some aspects of the fate of print logic in the early decades of new media. By "print logic," I mean the imagination of what Marshall McLuhan has described as the "Gutenberg Galaxy": the distinctive ways of thinking, knowing, and interacting with the world of letters that belong to such mighty institutions of print culture as the modern incarnations of the book, the library, the bookstore, and the newspaper.[7] As I argued in chapter 3, as scholars strive to make sense of the digital environment, they evade the trap of seeing digital forms as mere transformations of print technology; but as they strive to capture a piece of the emerging digital marketplace, they find themselves appealing to the frameworks of print culture. The marketplace also pushes for narratives of revolutionary change when they aren't called for; as in the context of critical analyses that are really trying to argue for the gradual character of media change, or in the promotion of products in which the new digital features may be superficial at best. The motivation for these narratives of change is in part commercial, fostered by the marketplace's zest for novelty; that is, we are having a media revolution in part simply because it is possible, because there is profit to be had in newness and in the resale of old content in new formats. On the other hand, digital spaces and communities really are changing the shape of literary practice. As audiences, we interact online in ways that we did not before; as producers of media content, we find ourselves mar-shalling skill sets that we did not before; as communities, we find ourselves colliding with a suite of norms, values, and practices, chronicled in *Wired* magazine and elsewhere, that had no part in the life of the intellectual in the great age of print.

The imperfect fit between print logic and print is an instance of the imperfect fit between culture and technology. In general, peo-ple don't resist technological change; they resist cultural change. Some commentators – I mentioned Adam Kirsch – have criticized the young discipline of the digital humanities on the basis that "humanistic work," that is, the work that scholars do with the aid of just a brain and a library, is a universal constant that doesn't change with technology. ("Was it necessary for a humanist in the past five hundred years to know how to set type and publish a book?" he asks.)[8] One of my professors in graduate school, a histo-rian who understood that the methods and culture of the human-ities do indeed change with technologies, nonetheless despised some aspects of digital pedagogy: "Not since the destruction of the monasteries by Henry VIII," he said unhappily, "have we been in such a period of feckless innovation." Both of these positions mount aggressive oppositions to the spectre of cultural change: one by refusing its very possibility, the other by comparing it with a famous cultural catastrophe. But the recognition that the objects of humanistic inquiry circulate in a new environment compels us to try to understand the values and practices of that environment – the most established kind of humanistic work.

## 2

Like many people in the university, I have been thinking a lot late-ly about professional values and cultural change. Alvin Kernan defines culture as "the complex, always-changing totality of activi-ties and beliefs, never entirely coherent, never totally objective, through and in which people organize life meaningfully and make their values real."[9] This includes the habits and values that one ac-quires as part of training within a profession or membership in a social group. To put it more simply, you are in a culture when, even if you don't know what to do, you know how to do it. Robert Darnton provides a memorable account of culture in this sense in a 1975 essay, "Writing News and Telling Stories," a memoir in which a cub reporter learns through rigorous initiation how to distinguish what counts as a story from what doesn't, how to write stories that editors will accept, and how to take mundane details from daily life and turn them into "news."[10] He also learns a value system that incorporates professional competition and newsroom hierarchy. Eventually, he is able to "read" the layout of a newsroom as a courtier would read the court of the Sun King, seeing a sign system of power, hierarchy, and prestige in the circulation of messages and the spacing of bodies:

> There are structural elements to the status system of the newsroom, as its layout indicates. The managing editor rules from within an office; and lesser editors command clusters of "desks" (foreign desk, national desk, city or 'metropolitan' desk) at one end of the room, an end that stands out by the different orientation of the furniture and that is enclosed behind a low fence. At the other end, row upon row of reporters' desks face the editors across the fence. They fall into four sections. First, a few rows of star reporters led by luminaries like Homer Bigart, Peter Kihss, and McCandlish Phillips. Then three rows of rewrite men, who sit to the side of the stars at the front of the room so that they can be near the command during deadline periods. Next, a spread of middle-aged veterans, men who have made their names and can be trusted with any story. And finally, a herd of young men on the make at the back of the room, the youngest generally occupying the remotest positions. Function determines some locations: sports, shipping, "culture," and "society" have their own corners; and copy readers sit accessibly to the side. But to the eye of the initiate, the general lines of the status system stand out as legibly as a banner headline.[11]

This is a "print" culture because it relies absolutely on print, existing for the purpose of putting out a daily print newspaper. It is also a culture whose most despotic characteristics have surprisingly little to do with print as a medium. That is what I mean by print culture: the institutions and frameworks of practice that we build around the existence of print, which may or may not take shape from the characteristics of print technology itself.

The new cultural communities that orbit the latest digital technologies have already attracted wide notice. The distinctive codes and habits of these communities may seem strange or even ridiculous to outsiders, but to insiders they constitute important expressions of values. Not long ago, I attended a wedding-slash-"maker faire" that emphasized its role as an expression of love between "makers." The event took place in the MIT Media Lab and was designed along the lines of a learning festival or maker faire, as the program below illustrates:

> If you're contributing to the potluck, *add your entry to the Potluck Tracker by* WEDNESDAY. Remember that dinner is a few hours after the event starts. We have a large kitchen with a fridge, freezers, counters and power sources – please add your needs to the spreadsheet. Thanks so much for sharing!
> Schedule for the Day (July 19th):
> - 3:00pm a brief ceremony
> - 3:40pm(ish): creative play
> - Johann Sebastian Joust (trailer)
> - Versability: the poetry game
> - Knitting
> - Stop-motion LEGO and Tinkertoy stations (no table flips plz!)
> - Invented board games
> - Learn polyvocal singing
> - Portrait studio
> - (likely) Space Team
> - (likely) Games for People
> - 6:00pm: potluck + catering
> - 7:30pm: dance and play the sun to sleep

Why Legos? Why knitting? Why learning stations and games? These are components in a specific occupational culture that the couple decided to celebrate as part of their union. Legos, which are small building blocks that can be combined and recombined into larger architectures, enjoy something like a mascot status in programming and engineering circles, as the dream at the heart of maker culture is to build new universes from grains of sand. (The Media Lab has large display tables of Legos for people to play with.) Collaboration is also a core value in "tech" culture, so it finds representation, for example, in the game Space Team, which has the explicit goal of teaching the players to work together as a team. The participants in the wedding reception understood that the games and stations were designed to promote sharing, collaboration, and DIY experimentation. As at college reunions, tailgates, and Phish concerts, part of what was being celebrated was socialization into a shared culture.

This event took its pattern from MIT's annual Festival of Learning and other maker institutions such as hackathons, DIY spaces, and maker faires like the one the White House recently hosted.[12] At these events, people gather to display, participate in, and celebrate a creative process that takes place through group work and the rapid, iterative construction of prototypes. Part of the goal of participating in such an event is to create, but part of the goal is also to become better socialized in a specific set of values and methods. This is why the communities that host hackathons and other events designed to create or improve real products also host more whimsical, but structurally similar, events such as the "cardboard challenge," an annual festival of building with corrugated paper.[13]

As with print culture, some of the distinctive habits of these cultures have nothing to do with the technologies they are meant to reflect. Of course, some habits do take their shape from technological affordances. For example, as Manovich and Benkler have argued, new media is inherently modular in structure, broken up into small units that can be assembled into larger entities; Lego builds, knitting projects, and hackathons, in which programmers work in mutual solitudes on different pieces of a software project, all reflect this logic in similar ways.[14] But glass walls, for example, which have no special connection to computer technologies, are a common feature of the spaces in which computer technologies are developed. Or again, a recent article in *Wired* reports that the

White House no longer expects the programmers who work there to "dress like adults."[15] Nothing in computer technologies demands that programmers dress in sneakers and hoodies, but it is an instantly recognizable part of the culture. When a twenty-one-year-old tech entrepreneur appeared, in 2014, on the cover of *Wired*, he showed his cultural credentials by wearing a hoodie.

Following the work of sociologists such as Verta Taylor, Nancy Whittier, Francesca Poletta, and James Jasper, we can register the process by which the digital revolution constitutes itself as a body of members.[16] The rituals, habits, and norms of the tech community set its members apart from the outside world, creating a framework of approaches and attitudes, methods and meanings, that are separate from mere technical knowledge but in practise tend to co-exist with it. In order to participate fully in the world of high-tech, a newcomer may justifiably feel obliged to undergo not just learning, but socialization.[17] This process may include attending shows and conferences, participating in the festivals, hackathons, and cardboard challenges that teach participants to build from modules and work in teams, and belonging to mailing lists whose members discuss technology issues, the better to pick things up from ambient chatter. Together, the world of gaming forums, hackathons, incubators, maker faires, and other hubs of digital socialization provides a space for cultural processes that distinguish insiders from outsiders. These are spaces that produce, in addition to technological literacies, cultural vocabularies, preferred brands and tastes, literacy in the prevailing narratives of one's field, and strong local knowledge. Participating in such specialized communities enables members to synchronize their behaviour and create shared narratives that make meaning of their actions. The so-called computer revolution, which is famously diffuse in its self-understanding, thus takes on specific habitations and names through shared rituals and symbols of belonging. Attending to this process can help us to better see the relationship – and the distinction – between the digital and the digerati.

The new culture even exhibits distinctive moral commitments. Langdon Winner, Fred Turner, Richard Barbrook, and others have contributed to a growing literature that identifies a distinctive set of ideologies with Silicon Valley.[18] Members of the technology avant-garde often display an attitude that observers have described as "techno-libertarian," characterized by a distrust of the state, disrespect for the law, and a faith in the ability of tools to solve problems of governance and social equity. They also have a taste for vigilante justice. Molly Sauter, a participant in "hacktivist" groups as well as an analyst of their methods, has written a sympathetic history of the use of DDOS attacks, in which a group covertly takes control of hundreds of civilian hard drives and uses them to overload an enemy's server with hits, as a method of activism or civil disobedience.[19] Or again, in 2010 the organization WikiLeaks threatened to release the contents of the hard drive of an executive at Bank of America.[20] The message – presumably something like "Sunlight is the best disinfectant" – may seem to some to be tainted by underhanded methods. But it resonates with the taste for vigilantism that hacktivist communities are observed to display.

Media scholars such as Luis Murillo, N. Katherine Hayles, and Kathleen Fitzpatrick have documented ways in which the social conditions of technologies shape their material forms and cultural meanings.[21] Communities that orbit cutting-edge technologies, like Murillo's hackers and Fitzpatrick's digital editors, can claim to participate in a "digital revolution" for reasons that are not merely technological, but cultural as well. The practices that define these communities exceed what the formal attributes of the technologies involved necessitate; indeed, precisely because collective identity supersedes local domains of practice, communities oriented around digital technology experience constant spillover between members. For example, the members of a new media discussion group might keep in touch by playing online computer games together, making them by definition members of a gamer community.

To return to a theme: people don't resist technological change; they resist cultural change. In their complicated response to the spread of computer technologies, what humanities departments are resisting, in large part, is a set of identity markers – values, habits, practices – that go with being in a computerized world. Humanists are trained to work alone; digital workers are trained to work in groups. Humanists are trained to analyze; digital workers are trained to create. Humanists are trained to dig deep and specialize in a single domain; digital workers are trained to move quickly and laterally. Humanists are trained to be anchors; digital workers are trained to be connectable nodes. Humanists are trained to dress "like adults"; digital workers are not. The differing repertoires of practice that these communities display even in shared spaces make this, in many ways, a case of languages divided by a common nation. Consider something as simple as protocol during an academic talk. At talks given before tech-oriented audiences, the use of communication technologies in the audience is common; some members of the audience may choose to exchange comments and gossip on an IRC backchannel while others take notes on public web documents. In audiences from classics and literature departments, however, to look at a screen during a talk is borderline impolite. Technological fluency, or at least fluency with a specific suite of communications technologies, attaches to one of these groups precisely because they identify as members of a tech-oriented audience.

This is a reason for humanists to embrace digital practice – even if doing so makes us feel more acutely what is being lost, even if we have been doing "humanistic work" quite ably for centuries without digital methods. If one mission of humanities departments is to manufacture humanists, then digital technologies, which open a rift between literacies that C.P. Snow never considered, place new demands upon the way we train students.[22] Public humanists in the next century will make steady use of new media tools and literacies. Already, the most interesting newspaper internships ask specifically for applicants who can perform data analysis. In politics, new media specialists working on campaigns, chief technology officers in city governments, civic media researchers at think tanks and non-profits, and members of bodies such as the White House Social and Behavioral Science Team require data literacy for the most mundane aspects of their work. In fact, literate citizenship in a world where governmental and administrative bodies increasingly boast of using "data-driven policy" requires computational literacies that a liberal arts education has not previously demanded. We should build those skills into a humanistic education simply because those skills now belong to humanistic production; and the best way to prepare ourselves to build those skills into a humanistic education is to build them into our own work as researchers. Students in the humanities need to practise working in groups, designing and reshaping tools, moving back and forth between theoretical problems and design problems, and other practices that belong to the social world of information technology. This is not just a matter of curriculum change in universities, but also a matter of changes in the social and cultural fabric of the humanities.

3

All of this is a way of explaining why I have tended, in this book, to focus on points of distinction from, rather than similarities with, other media ecosystems. This choice of priorities is partly tactical, a way of advocating for a shifted discourse; it also accentuates the necessity to expand our genealogies. The potential for new media to foster new creative communities is immediately visible in the distinctive ways in which the people who produce new media come together, such as hackathons, maker faires, rapid prototyping workshops, "black hat" meetings, tech talks, industry demos, project shares, and "studios" and "labs." We can see that these spaces shape the products that emerge from them, and we can directly see the importance of social over individual influences. As Manovich discusses, the rise of media software changed the media avant-garde from "individuals in studios" to "a variety of players, from very big to very small"; the rise of a productive model in which interdisciplinary teamwork, not specialized labour, reigns, as well as the fact that the new players include engineers, programmers, and other hackers and makers, has important implications for our understanding of contemporary media art.[23] These agents interact and build communities of practice in ways peculiar to themselves and not to other artists: for example, in the spaces of collaboration listed above.[24] The social dynamics that govern the environments in which digital tools arise differ from those of earlier media systems; so too do the social dynamics that govern online environments. An understanding of either requires attention to the formal properties of tools and interfaces, but also careful attention to the social dynamics of communities.

It can be tempting to elide these differences, when discussing activity within media environments, in favour of seeking out what they have in common – in the pursuit of universal cultural formations. Storytelling is one example of such a concept that has attracted attention in many different branches of the humanities. Distinguishing storytelling from specific media forms (and their material and cultural substructures) has the advantage of allowing us to ask what global uses we have made of media. In his book *The Storytelling Animal*, Jonathan Gottschall offers reasons for viewing storytelling as an adaptive evolutionary characteristic: stories find or create "meaningful patterns in the world," helping us to cope with the world in which we find ourselves; stories favour conflict and danger, enabling us to imagine our way through problems; stories tend more often to endure when they convey moral lessons, making them aids to social cohesion.[25] Nevertheless, the concept of storytelling has limited utility when the goal is to identify consequences of media change. Gottschall has written elsewhere of storytelling as a cultural constant: "For humans, story is like gravity: an inescapable field of force that influences everything, but is so omnipresent that we hardly notice it."[26] But my goal is precisely to make distinctions between different cultural formations – to see, so to speak, not gravity, but rather what's happening on the ground.

For the same reason, a generalizing term much favoured in game studies – play – has limited utility for this situation. As Brian Sutton-Smith notes in *The Ambiguity of Play* (2001), almost any activity will admit the concept of play under its aegis; scholars have discussed daydreaming, television, tourism, sex, and even gossip as forms of play.[27] Literature, too (even storytelling, if you prefer), is undoubtedly a form of play, and as such, the practice of writing stories for fanfiction sites (for example) and the practice of writing stories for print have important motivations in common. Yet examining these sites as a distinctive literary ecosystem enables us to better consider the ways in which fanfiction evades traditional values of "literary" authorship such as inspiration, originality, and uniqueness. Even if we agree that fanfiction authors are authors in a Barthesian sense, it makes a difference that they are also game players; as a starting point, they are observably more productive authors because they are game players.

The interest of this book has therefore been in distinctions, not unities – distinctions that provide grounds for better understanding specialized systems of social and literary activity. The effect of game mechanics on fanfiction websites, for example, suggests that communities of writing and reading on the Web are already working out distinctive ways of circulating and understanding texts. To that end, this book has attempted to show the value of teasing out the game elements in a larger online culture that emphasizes voluntary, free activity. In many digital textual cultures, the conditions of the production and reception of texts differ so thoroughly from their former existence that it changes the text's field of activity altogether, moving our "textual condition" away from the cultural "logics" of print media, although print media continues to inform the interface metaphor we use for online platforms, and toward game play.

Ultimately, this book has attempted to show the value of expanding our genealogies of digital textuality. As I said in chapter 2, the idea that textual production shares a direct lineage with games has not previously been a part of the self-understanding of the humanities. An understanding of the digital medium in terms of multiple histories has attracted growing interest among historians, following for example the groundbreaking work of Michael Mahoney, or Jonathan Zittrain's discussion of the "digital ecosystem" as an arena for many different fields of activity.[28] This creates a distinctive problem in historiography: as historians now recognize, the "history" of computing is in fact a suite of histories reflecting the goals, methods, and experiences of different communities. Sometimes communities at the centre of the computing world move to the periphery or vanish, such that their histories no longer provide a direct genealogy for our digital practice; at other times, as with the rise of gamification, communities of practice at the periphery move to the centre. This is not just a matter of new technologies; more important is a corresponding change in attitudes, on the part of the creators and users of online textual platforms, that makes it difficult to imagine a disciplinary core that flows directly back to the history of the book. Today, the discipline that has come to be known as the digital humanities encompasses too much activity, incorporates too many histories, to trace back a single genealogy for its protean operations.[29] The task now before us is to incorporate, into our teaching and research, histories that have not previously belonged to the histories of humanistic activity. We have only begun to investigate these new configurations.

# Notes

## Introduction

1 The term "second-order reality" is from Roger Callois, *Man, Play and Games* (Chicago: University of Illinois Press, 1958).

2 The term *Web 2.0*, used to describe a new class of technologies that transformed the web into a read-write platform, allowing readers to share and comment on content, was coined in 1999 and popularized in 2004. Following the rise of Web 2.0, web-based services took increasing interest in methods to promote user-to-user interactivity. In 2003, a game developer named Nick Pelling coined the term *gamification* to describe one such method: the embedding of game mechanics into other kinds of activities. The next chapter addresses debates over gamification in industry and game studies.

3 For example, an Italian book of parlour games published in 1551 suggests a game in which the members of a gathering each produce a poem or a similar text; the gathering will judge the poems together, and a player who has been appointed "president" will deal out rewards and punishments. Another book remarks, "Like laboratories for assaying and refining precious metals, parlour games are true proving grounds for experimenting with 'wit,' 'wisdom,' and 'skill.'" George McClure, *Parlour Games and the Public Life of Women in Renaissance Italy* (Toronto: University of Toronto Press, 2013), 25.

4 José van Dijck, *The Culture of Connectivity: A Critical History of Social Media* (Oxford: Oxford University Press, 2013). Her term for the

hermetic environment of a specific platform is *microsystem*, which I also use.

5  Van Dijck treats YouTube as a social media site "because communities share specific postings"; I do the same in this book, although I do not discuss YouTube at length. Ibid., 9.

6  As I will argue in later chapters, these features are implemented, in large part, to serve the purpose of keeping users actively engaged with their screens. For example, van Dijck notes that the photo-sharing platform Flickr has often "foregrounded coding features that accentuate newsiness and transience," at one point including "buttons to view 'Interesting photos from the last 7 days' and 'Most recent uploads' as well as an automated teller of 'Uploads in the last minute', all intended to boost traffic and generate interest in current affairs." Ibid., 93. The emphasis on newness, liveness, and continual activity that these buttons implement both embellish the platforms as game systems and serve the economic interests of the platform owners.

7  Ibid., 9–10.

8  Facebook Internet Stats, accessed 18 July 2017, http://www.internet worldstats.com/facebook.htm; van Dijck, *The Culture of Connectivity*, 45. The figures that I provide represent an update from van Dijck's figures, which are from the same source.

9  Van Dijck, *The Culture of Connectivity*, 45–9.

10 Raph Koster defines game mechanics as "rule based systems/ simulations that facilitate and encourage a user to explore and learn the properties of their possibility space through the use of feedback mechanisms." He cautions readers, however, that feedback alone does not constitute game mechanics; these rule-based systems and feedback mechanisms must be incorporated into larger *game systems*. I discuss traditional definitions of such systems, and their relation to features of specific online platforms, in the next chapter. Raph Koster, "Feedback Does Not Equal Game Design," *Raph Koster* (blog), 4 January 2011, accessed 18 July 2017, https://www.raphkoster.com/2011/01/04/feedback-does-not-equal-game-design/.

11 In the next section, I explain why I attend to *Archive of Our Own*, a "fan" platform.

12 On the complex relationship between narrative and database, see, for example, N. Katherine Hayles, *How We Think: Digital Media and Contemporary Technogenesis* (Chicago: University of Chicago Press, 2012), 171–248; and the collection of essays in "Special Topic: Remapping Genre," *PMLA* 122, no. 5 (October 2007). The first discussion of this pairing appears in Lev Manovich, *The Language of New Media* (Cambridge, MA: MIT Press, 2001).

13 Steven Hetcher, "Amateur Creative Digital Content and Proportional Commerce," in *Amateur Media: Social, Cultural, and Legal Perspectives*, ed. Dan Hunter, Ramon Lobato, Megan Richardson, and Julian Thomas (London: Routledge, 2013), 38.

14 Karen Hellekson, "A Fannish Field of Value: Online Fan Gift Culture," *Cinema Journal* 48, no. 4 (Summer 2009): 114. She adds, "Fan communities as they are currently comprised, require exchanges of gifts: you do not pay to read fanfiction or watch a fan-made music vid. They are offered for free (although circulation may be restricted and you may have to know where to obtain them), yet within a web of context that specifies an appropriate mode of 'payment.'"

15 Andrew Keen, *The Cult of the Amateur: How Today's Internet Is Killing Our Culture* (New York: Doubleday, 2007), 17. Keen's book is cited in Hetcher, "Amateur Creative Digital Content," 38.

16 Hetcher, "Amateur Creative Digital Content," 39–40.

## Chapter One

1 Alexander Galloway, "The Unworkable Interface," *New Literary History* 39 (2009): 933.

2 See, for example, Jerome McGann, *The Textual Condition* (Princeton: Princeton University Press, 1991).

3 See, for example, Alvin Kernan, *The Imaginary Library: An Essay on Literature and Society* (Princeton: Princeton University Press, 1982); and Alvin Kernan, *Samuel Johnson and the Impact of Print* (1987; repr., Princeton: Princeton University Press, 1989). Of course, it is by now a commonplace of media studies and textual scholarship that

"print logic," in Kernan's term, does not exist as an intrinsic property of the technology of print. But scholars equally recognize that, although there is no definite logic of print, there are definite logics, however circumscribed in place and time, that belong to the social institutions of print media – embedded, for example, in the occupational training of journalists, the organization of publishing houses, the self-regulation of academic disciplines, and the battlefield strategizing of librarians in their perpetual war against chaos. On this point, see, for example, J.A. Dane, *The Myth of Print Culture: Essays on Evidence, Textuality, and Bibliographical Method* (Toronto: University of Toronto Press, 2003).

4  See, for example, Ilana Snyder, ed., *Page to Screen: Taking Literacy into the Electronic Era* (New York: Routledge, 2003); Peter Stoicheff and Andrew Taylor, *The Future of the Page* (Toronto: University of Toronto Press, 2004); William Powers, *Hamlet's Blackberry: A Practical Philosophy for Building a Good Life in the Digital Age* (New York: Scribe Publications, 2010); and, for an account that considers the roles of the physical and electronic page in the composition process, Matthew Kirschenbaum, *Track Changes: A Literary History of Word Processing* (Cambridge, MA: Harvard University Press, 2016).

5  This claim extends the terms, of course, of a growing practical awareness of the role of *liveness* in our response to digital texts. To give a prominent example, José van Dijck comments of Twitter, or specifically of Twitter's corporate ambition and popular reputation, that "what is new in microblogging is that the tweet flow … is conceptualized as a *live* stream of uninhibited, unedited, instant, short, and short-lived reactions – a stream that supposedly taps a *real-time* undercurrent of opinions and gut feelings." José van Dijck, *The Culture of Connectivity: A Critical History of Social Media* (Oxford: Oxford University Press, 2013), 78 (emphasis in original). Twitter has further connected this emphasis on liveness to its core business as the company has sought, more recently, "to strategically position itself in the market of predictive analytics and real-time analytics," partnering with analytics scientists who are able to convert "live" user-generated data into predictive tools, saleable information, and better tools for tracking and advertising. Ibid., 80–7. Other signs of this awareness are the popular use of the names of successful digital

communication platforms (although not exclusively social-media platforms) as verbs – skyping, tweeting – and the habit, in Silicon Valley, of giving apps designed for use with these platforms names that sound like adverbs. See, for example, "Names that End in -ly," *Pinterest*, which as of 4 August 2016 catalogues 284 examples of technology brand names that end in "-ly."

6  Kenneth Goldsmith, "Why I Am Teaching a Course Called 'Wasting Time on the Internet,'" *New Yorker*, 13 November 2014, accessed 18 July 2017, http://www.newyorker.com/books/page-turner/wasting-time-on-the-internet.

7  Barbara H. Kwasnik, "A Descriptive Study of the Functional Components of Browsing," *School of Information Studies Faculty Scholarship*, paper 142 (1992). Kwasnik summarizes the foundational literature on browsing activity as follows: "In this sense, browsing emphasizes sudden insight, hitherto unrecognized relationships (Apted, 1971) and 'lateral thinking' (DeBono, 1970), in which the process of navigating through information is perhaps in itself more valuable than getting an answer; where information is used for its effects rather than for its own sake (what we call heuristics); where we might seek out the irrelevant in an attempt to 'shake up' the existing conceptual structures; where ambiguity is sought out rather than rejected; and where the process is generative rather than selective, that is, the process of finding information creates new patterns of knowledge (Bawden, 1986; DeBono, 1970; O'Connor, 1988)." She also notes that many digital information systems explicitly design browsing into their functionality.

8  James Paradis, personal communication, 20 January 2014.

9  Bernard Cerquiglini, *In Praise of the Variant: A Critical History of Philology*, trans. Betsy Wing (1989; repr., Baltimore: Johns Hopkins University Press, 1999).

10  See, for example, Jonathan Zittrain, Kendra Albert, and Lawrence Lessig, "Perma: Scoping and Addressing the Problem of Link and Reference Rot in Legal Citations" (working paper no. 13–42, Harvard Law Review Forum, Cambridge, 2013).

11  See, for example, Mary Flanagan, *Critical Play: Radical Game Design* (Cambridge, MA: MIT Press, 2009), and John Sharp, *Works of Game: On the Aesthetics of Games and Art* (Cambridge, MA: MIT Press, 2015).

12 Michael Groden, *"Ulysses" in Focus: Genetic, Textual, and Personal Views* (Gainesville, FL: University Press of Florida, 2010), 7.

13 Susan Schreibman, "The Versioning Machine," *Literary and Linguistic Computing* 18, no. 1 (2001): 101–7. See also, for example, Richard J. Finneran, *The Literary Text in the Digital Age* (Ann Arbor, MI: University of Michigan Press, 1996); Jerome McGann, *Radiant Textuality: Literature after the World Wide Web* (New York: Palgrave McMillan, 2001); Daniel Apollon, Claire Bélisle, and Philippe Régnier, eds, *Digital Critical Editions* (Urbana, IL: University of Illinois Press, 2014).

14 Kathleen Fitzpatrick, *Planned Obsolescence: Publishing, Technology, and the Future of the Academy* (New York: New York University Press, 2011); and Susan Schreibman, "The Versioning Machine," accessed 18 July 2017, v-machine.org.

15 McGann also emphasizes in *Radiant Textuality* the mutual influence of libraries and digitization initiatives in stimulating the development of fluid, version-oriented textual archives. McGann, *Radiant Textuality*, 3.

16 Kernan, *Samuel Johnson and the Impact of Print*, 245–6.

17 See, for example, Fitzpatrick, *Planned Obsolescence*; N. Katherine Hayles, *How We Think: Digital Media and Contemporary Technogenesis* (Chicago: University of Chicago Press, 2012); N. Katherine Hayles, *My Mother Was a Computer: Digital Subjects and Literary Texts* (Chicago: University of Chicago Press, 2005); Johanna Drucker, *SpecLab: Digital Aesthetics and Projects in Speculative Computing* (Chicago: University of Chicago Press, 2009).

18 See, for example, van Dijck, *The Culture of Connectivity*; Christian Fuchs, *Culture and Economy in the Age of Social Media* (New York: Routledge, 2015); and Tarleton Gillespie, "The Politics of Platforms," *New Media and Society* 12, no. 3 (2010): 347–64.

19 For example: "Traditional scholarship operates through a complex machinery of paper-based social software about which digital technicians are often deeply ignorant. The ontologies needed to organize an effective online educational system are already operating, largely transparently, within the social network of traditional scholarship and education. The Machine of the Book, perhaps the greatest social technology ever invented, should be the object of deep

study by human-interface designers"; Jerome McGann, *The New Republic of Letters: Memory and Scholarship in the Age of Digital Reproduction* (Cambridge, MA: Harvard University Press, 2014), 145. To underscore the extent to which McGann relies rhetorically on a history of digital texts that leads back to traditional bibliography, although he acknowledges the differences between them, here are some terms he uses in the first six pages: "textual machines" (1); "the complex machineries of books" (1), "technology of books" (1), "bibliographical technology" (1), "book technology" (4), "textual machine" (5), and "amazing technology" (in reference to the critical scholarly edition) (6).

20  McGann, *The New Republic of Letters*, 46.

21  David Weinberger, *Too Big to Know: Rethinking Knowledge Now That the Facts Aren't the Facts, Experts Are Everywhere, and the Smartest Person in the Room Is the Room* (New York: Basic Books, 2012).

22  McGann, *The New Republic of Letters*, 43.

23  Robert Coover, "Literary Hypertext: The Passing of the Golden Age" (keynote, Digital Arts and Culture, 29 October 1999).

24  McGann, *The Textual Condition*, 22.

25  Henry Jenkins, *Textual Poachers: Television Fans & Participatory Culture* (New York: Routledge, 2002).

26  Abigail De Kosnik, "Fandom as Free Labor," in *Digital Labor: The Internet as Playground and Factory*, ed. Trebor Scholz (New York: Routledge, 2013), 98.

27  Anne Elizabeth Jamison, ed., *Fic: Why Fanfiction Is Taking over the World* (Dallas: BenBella Books, 2013).

28  I use the term "modding" to refer to all fan modifications of computer games, but Hector Postigo breaks down the activity in a more detailed taxonomy: "modders" alter the game's physics, storyline, or game type; "mappers" design new game levels; "skinners" design new characters; and weapons makers design new tools. Hector Postigo, "Of Mods and Modders: Chasing Down the Value of Fan-Based Digital Game Modifications," *Games and Culture* 2, no. 4 (October 2007): 301.

29  Julian Kücklich, "Precarious Playbour: Modders and the Digital Games Industry," *Fibreculture Journal* 5 (2005), accessed 18 July 2017,

http://five.fibreculturejournal.org/fcj-025-precarious-playbour-modders-and-the-digital-games-industry/. See also Stephen Kline, Nick Dyer-Witheford, and Greig de Peuter, *Digital Play: The Interaction of Technology, Culture and Marketing* (Montreal: McGill-Queen's University Press, 2003); Eric Champion, *Game Mods: Design, Theory, and Criticism* (New York: ETC Press, 2012); and David Kushner, "The Mod Squad," *Popular Science*, 2 July 2002, accessed 18 July 2017, http://www.popsci.com/gear-gadgets/article/2002-07/mod-squad.

30 While some modders find employment in the game industry, most do not translate modding into employment. Hector Postigo, "Modding to the Big Leagues: Exploring the Space between Modders and the Game Industry," *First Monday*, 5 May 2010, accessed 18 July 2017, http://journals.uic.edu/ojs/index.php/fm/article/view/2972/0. See also Postigo, "Of Mods and Modders," 300–13; Abe Stein, "Televisual Sports Videogames" (Master's thesis, Massachusetts Institute of Technology, 2013); and Wagner James Au, "Triumph of the Mod," *Salon*, 16 April 2002, accessed 18 July 2017, http://www.salon.com/2002/04/16/modding/.

31 Kücklich, "Precarious Playbour."

32 Ibid. Kücklich means that modding and similar activities do not fit solely within any of these categories.

33 De Kosnik, "Fandom as Free Labor," 99. See also Abigail De Kosnik, *Rogue Archives: Digital Cultural Memory and Media Fandom* (Cambridge, MA: MIT Press, 2016), especially 27, 51–6.

34 Manuel Castells is the most famous theorist of the "network society." I draw, here, on his accounts of a rising economy based on creativity, "flexible production," and "informational" labour. See, for example, Manuel Castells, *The Rise of the Network Society* (Oxford: Blackwell Publishers, 1996).

35 De Kosnik, "Fandom as Free Labor," 103.

36 Ibid.

37 Matthew Hills, *Fan Cultures* (New York: Routledge, 2002), 5.

38 Ibid., 10.

39 Richard Barbrook, "The Hi-tech Gift Economy," *First Monday*, 5 December 2005, accessed 18 July 2017, http://journals.uic.edu/ojs/index.php/fm/article/view/631.

40 See also Tiziana Terranova, "Free Labor," in *Digital Labor: The Internet as Playground and Factory*, ed. Trebor Scholz (New York: Routledge, 2013): 33–57.

41 Marcel Mauss, *The Gift: The Form and Reason for Exchange in Archaic Societies*, trans. W.D. Halls (New York and London: W.W. Norton, 1990). Originally published as "Essai sur le Don. Forme et Raison de l'Echange dans les Sociétés archaïques," *L'Année sociologique* 1 (1923–24): 30–186.

42 Utopian visions of the Web share many threads but also reflect multiple motives and communities of practice. Fred Turner discusses the merging, in the second half of the twentieth century, of cyberculture with the American counterculture, and through this merger "the rise of digital utopianism." Fred Turner, *From Counterculture to Cyberculture: Stewart Brand, the Whole Earth Network* (Chicago: The University of Chicago Press, 2006). José van Dijck, meanwhile, discusses the relationship between the realities of social media and "early utopian visions of the Web as a space that inherently enhances social activity." Van Dijck, *The Culture of Connectivity*, 13. Jeff Jarvis is an example of a media critic who celebrates the humanizing potential of the "new industry based on sharing." Jeff Jarvis, *Public Parts: How Sharing in the Digital Age Improves the Way We Work and Live* (New York: Simon & Schuster, 2011).

43 See, for example, Walter Ong, "Writing Is a Technology that Restructures Thought," in *The Written Word: Literacy in Transition*, ed. Gerd Bauman (Oxford: Oxford University Press, 1986), 23–50.

44 See, for example, Yochai Benkler, *The Wealth of Networks: How Social Production Transforms Markets and Freedom* (New Haven, CT: Yale University Press, 2006).

45 Barbrook, "The Hi-tech Gift Economy."

46 Ibid.

47 Terranova, "Free Labor."

48 Ultimately, the Department of Labor chose not to pursue the case. Hector Postigo, "Emerging Sources of Labor on the Internet: The Case of America Online Volunteers," in *Uncovering Labour in Information Revolutions, 1750–2000*, ed. Aad Blok and Greg Downey (Cambridge: Cambridge University Press, 2003), 205. Lisa Napoli,

"Former Volunteers Sue AOL, Seeking Back Pay for Work," *New York Times*, 26 May 1999, accessed 18 July 2017, http://www.nytimes.com /1999/05/26/nyregion/former-volunteers-sue-aol-seeking-back-pay-for-work.html. The *Times* article says AOL identified itself as having 10,000 volunteers.

49 Tiziana Terranova, *Network Culture: Politics for the Information Age* (London: Pluto, 2004), 47–8.

50 Terranova, "Free Labor," 33. Further discussions of free labour online as a form of exploitation include Soren Mork Petersen, "Loser Generated Content: From Participation to Exploitation," *First Monday* 13, no. 3 (3 March 2008), accessed 18 July 2017, http://www.firstmonday .dk/ojs/index.php/fm/article/view/2141/1948; and, in an account that is more descriptivist than prescriptivist, Christian Fuchs, "The Digital Labour Theory of Value and Karl Marx in the Age of Facebook, YouTube, Twitter, and Weibo," in *Reconsidering Value and Labour in the Digital Age*, ed. Christian Fuchs and Eran Fisher (New York: Palgrave, 2015), 26–41.

51 Andrew Ross, "In Search of the Lost Paycheck," in *Digital Labor: The Internet as Playground and Factory*, ed. Trebor Scholz (New York: Routledge, 2013), 13–32.

52 Daniel Roth, "The Answer Factory: Demand Media and the Fast, Disposable, Portable as Hell Media Model," *Wired*, 19 October 2009, accessed 18 July 2017, https://www.wired.com/2009/10/ff _demandmedia/.

53 "LEAKED: AOL's Master Plan," *Business Insider*, 11 February 2011, accessed 18 July 2017, http://www.businessinsider.com/the-aol-way.

54 The article that coined the term "crowdsourcing" was Jeff Howe, "The Rise of Crowdsourcing," *Wired* 14, no. 6 (June 2006): 1–4. For an incisive analysis of *Wired* magazine's "political vision," see Langdon Winner, "Peter Pan in Cyberspace: *Wired* Magazine's Political Vision," *Educom Review* 30, no. 3 (May–June 1995), accessed 18 July 2017, https://net.educause.edu/apps/er/review/reviewArticles /30318.html.

55 See, for example, Don Tapscott and Anthony B. Williams, *Wikinomics: How Mass Collaboration Changes Everything* (New York: Penguin, 2006); and Clay Shirky, *Cognitive Surplus: Creativity and Generosity in a Connected Age* (New York: Penguin Press, 2010).

56 Rebecca Tushnet, "Legal Fictions: Copyright, Fan Fiction, and a New Common Law," *Loyola of Los Angeles Entertainment Law Journal* 17 (1997): 638. Quoted in David Tan, "Harry Potter and the Transformation Wand: Fair Use, Canonicity and Fan Activity," in *Amateur Media: Social and Legal Perspectives*, ed. Dan Hunter, Ramon Lobato, Megan Richardson, and Julian Thomas (New York: Routledge, 2013), 97. See also Jenkins, *Textual Poachers*; and Jeff Bishop and Paul Hoggett, *Organizing Around Enthusiasms: Mutual Aid in Leisure* (London: Comedia, 1986).

57 Eric Zimmerman and Katie Salen, *Rules of Play: Game Design Fundamentals* (Cambridge, MA: MIT Press, 2004), 67.

58 Ross, "In Search of the Lost Paycheck," 16–19.

59 See Alison Hearn, "Structuring Feeling: Web 2.0, Online Ranking and Rating, and the Digital 'Reputation' Economy," *ephemera: theory & politics in organization* 10, no. 3 (August 2010): 421–38.

60 Quoted in Ross, "In Search of the Lost Paycheck," 18.

61 Kernan, *Samuel Johnson and the Impact of Print*, 12.

62 For a discussion of this literature in the context of the larger history of information management, see Ann Blair, *Too Much to Know: Managing Scholarly Information before the Modern Age* (New Haven: Yale University Press, 2010).

## Chapter Two

1 Ian Bogost, "Gamification Is Bullshit," *Atlantic*, 9 August 2011, accessed 18 July 2017, https://www.theatlantic.com/technology /archive/2011/08/gamification-is-bullshit/243338/. Bogost adds, "Unlike liars, bullshitters have no use for the truth," but Frankfurt's point is that bullshitters have exactly as much use for the truth as they do for lies. They base the choice between truth and lies on which will be more effective. See Harry G. Frankfurt, *On Bullshit* (Princeton: Princeton University Press, 2005).

2 Recent industry-friendly books on the subject include Jane McGonigal, *Reality Is Broken: Why Games Make Us Better and How They Can Change the World* (New York: Penguin Press, 2011); Brian Burke, *Gamify: How Gamification Motivates People to do Extraordinary Things* (Brookline, MA: Bibliomotion, 2014); and Gabe Zichermann and

Christopher Cunningham, *Gamification by Design: Implementing Game Mechanics in Web and Mobile Apps* (Cambridge, MA: O'Reilly Media, Inc., 2011).

3 Bogost, "Gamification Is Bullshit."

4 Writers of business books, who have a stake in emphasizing the benefits of their advice, may add to this definition a goal of user engagement; for example, Gabe Zichermann and Christopher Cunningham define gamification as "the process of game-thinking and game mechanics to engage users and solve problems." Zichermann and Cunningham, *Gamification by Design*, xiv.

5 Ian Bogost, *Persuasive Games: The Expressive Power of Videogames* (Cambridge, MA: MIT Press, 2007).

6 Ian Bogost, "Persuasive Games: Exploitationware," *Gamasutra.com*, 3 May 2011, accessed 18 July 2017, http://www.gamasutra.com/view /feature/134735/persuasive_games_exploitationware.php. To combat the "rhetorical power" of the term gamification, Bogost has proposed that we use term exploitationware to describe this practice in corporate contexts. I have no problem with this change in rhetoric, if it makes speakers feel more comfortable.

7 Bogost, "Gamification Is Bullshit."

8 Bogost, "Persuasive Games: Exploitationware."

9 An account of a recent attempt by the Joyce scholar Joe Nugent to translate *Ulysses* into a computer game, along with the challenges this entails, appears in Elyse Graham, "*Ulysses*: The Video Game," *American Scholar* (5 December 2016), accessed 18 July 2017.

10 "In particular, gamification proposes to replace real incentives with fictional ones. Real incentives come at a cost but provide value for both parties based on a relationship of trust. By contrast, pretend incentives reduce or eliminate costs, but in so doing they strip away both value and trust." Bogost, "Persuasive Games: Exploitationware." See also Heather Chaplin, "I Don't Want to Be a Superhero," *Slate*, 29 March 2011, accessed 18 July 2017, http://www.slate.com/articles /technology/gaming/2011/03/i_dont_want_to_be_a_superhero.html.

11 Espen Aarseth, "Genre Trouble: Narrativism and the Art of Simulation," in *First Person: New Media as Story, Performance, and Game*, ed. P. Harrington and N. Wardrip-Fruin (Cambridge, MA: MIT Press, 2004): 45–7; Makku Eskelinen, "The Gaming Situation," *Game Studies* 1, no.

1 (2001), accessed 18 July 2017, http://www.gamestudies.org/0101
/eskelinen/.

12 "The [video game] industry posted an estimated $34.2 billion in rev-
enue in 2012, and revenue is expected to grow at an average of 5.5%
over the next five years." Jordan Weaver et al., "The Impact of Video
Games on Student GPA, Study Habits, and Time Management Skills:
What's the Big Deal?" *Issues in Information Systems* 14, no. 1 (2013):
122. In 2014, total consumer spending on the games industry (video
and computer games) was $22.41 billion. Entertainment Software
Association, "Essential Facts about the Computer Game Industry"
(2015): 13, accessed 18 July 2017, http://www.theesa.com/wp-content
/uploads/2015/04/ESA-Essential-Facts-2015.pdf. In 2004, Espen
Aarseth described the sense of rapid disciplinary growth that game
scholarship was experiencing: "In the last few years, games have
gone from media non grata to a recognized field of great scholarly
potential, a place for academic expansion and recognition. The great
stake-claiming race is on." Aarseth, "Genre Trouble," 45.

13 Ludwig Wittgenstein, *Philosophical Investigations* (1953; repr., Oxford:
Blackwell, 1997), 31–2.

14 Bernard Suits, *Grasshopper: Games, Life, and Utopia* (Toronto: University of Toronto Press, 1978), 3.

15 Katie Salen and Eric Zimmerman, *Rules of Play: Game Design Fundamentals* (Cambridge, MA: MIT Press, 2004), 80.

16 In his famous study of play, *Homo Ludens*, the historian Johan
Huizinga termed this last element "the magic circle." Johan Huizin-
ga, *Homo Ludens: A Study of the Play-Element in Culture* (Boston: The
Beacon Press, 1955), 10.

17 James Carse gives an excellent explanation for this intuition by distinguishing between finite and infinite games. Finite games have an
objective, an ending, an outcome, and rules that remain static within
the span of a given game, whereas infinite games have no objective,
no ending, no outcome, and rules that shift in order to prevent an
outcome from being reached: "A finite game is played for the purpose of winning, an infinite game for the purpose of continuing the
game." *Tetris* is an example of an infinite game – I borrow the example from Jane McGonigal – because when we play *Tetris*, our objective is not to win, but to prolong the game. James Carse, *Finite and*

*Infinite Games* (New York: The Free Press, 1986), 3; McGonigal, *Reality Is Broken*, 41.

18 To be sure, the platform produces something useful in the sense that we can use Facebook, for example, to find an apartment or conduct research. But Facebook was not designed for these purposes; it was designed, and is largely used, as a social-media and content distribution platform. Furthermore, as I discuss below, the points system that the "like" button and its corollaries constitute produces nothing outside of the space of the platform.

19 They must lose their way deliberately, because Facebook follows the norm, in contemporary website design, of organizing the page in order to emphasize clear usability and readability. On the norm of usability in contemporary website design, see, for example, Steve Krug, *Don't Make Me Think, Revisited: A Common Sense Approach to Web Usability* (San Francisco, CA: New Riders, 2014).

20 On the ideological inscriptions that accompany print newspaper layouts, see, for example, Robert Darnton, "Writing News and Telling Stories," *Daedalus* 104 (1975): 177. On printed facebooks, see, for example, Elyse Graham, "When Facebook Came to Princeton," *Princeton Alumni Weekly* (1 June 2016), accessed 18 July 2017, https://paw .princeton.edu/article/when-facebook-came-princeton.

21 These conventions also emphasize the role of professional gatekeepers in judging the importance of stories.

22 Kenneth Goldsmith, "Why I Am Teaching a Course Called 'Wasting Time on the Internet,'" *New Yorker*, 13 November 2014, accessed 18 July 2017, http://www.newyorker.com/books/page-turner/wasting-time-on-the-internet; Kenneth Goldsmith, *Wasting Time on the Internet* (New York: Harper Perennial, 2016). Henry Jenkins offers a classic analysis of media integration on digital platforms in Henry Jenkins, *Convergence Culture: Where Old and New Media Collide* (New York: New York University Press, 2006).

23 Jennifer Romano Bergstrom and Andrew Jonathan Schall, *Eye Tracking in User Experience Design* (Waltham, MA: Elsevier Inc., 2014).

24 Alexander Galloway, *Protocol: How Control Exists after Decentralization* (Cambridge, MA: MIT Press, 2004); Lawrence Lessig, *Code: And Other Laws of Cyberspace, Version 2.0* (New York: Basic Books, 2006).

25 Sharelle M. Burt, "The Power of the Hashtag: Top 10 Hashtags of

2015," *New York Daily News*, 21 December 2015, accessed 18 July 2017, http://www.nydailynews.com/news/national/power-hashtag-top-10-hashtags-2015-article-1.2463053.

26 The uptake of ideas and fads in the digital world has attracted a large literature under the rubric of memes, a term that Richard Dawkins originally devised to describe the spread of non-biological entities, such as ideas, in a manner reminiscent of natural selection. Ian Hacking, *Historical Ontology* (Cambridge, MA: Harvard University Press, 2002); Richard Dawkins, *The Selfish Gene* (Oxford: Oxford University Press, 1976).

27 Facebook recently expanded the functionality of the "like" button to include a palette of six emoticons: "Like," "Love," "Haha," "Wow," "Sad," and "Angry." Zichermann and Cunningham would say that this change fits entirely within the tactics of gamification. The palette of like options gives the feedback that likes constitute the element of surprise; the user does not know exactly what emoticons will appear among the likes. Slot machines work by a similar principle. Zichermann and Cunningham, *Gamification by Design*, 18–19.

28 A Google search on 24 July 2016 for "tips Facebook 'more likes'" returned 744,000 results; the first results page consisted entirely of websites offering tips for boosting one's likes and comments on Facebook.

29 I "won the Internet" once. It was thrilling.

30 "The feedback system tells players how close they are to achieving the goal. It can take the form of points, levels, a score, or a progress bar. Or, in its most basic form, the feedback system can be as simple as the players' knowledge of an objective outcome: 'The game is over when … ' Real-time feedback serves as a promise to the players that the goal is definitely achievable, and it provides motivation to keep playing." McGonigal, *Reality Is Broken*, 21.

31 Ibid., 24.

32 Ibid.

33 Ibid., 24–5.

34 Of course, there exist institutions, like libraries, that have the purpose of helping to preserve books. However, their existence does not guide the layout and mechanics of the print page in the thorough-

going way that I am describing here. Provided that it is printed on acid-free paper, a book will survive nearly as well in a dry chest as it will in a library.

35 I haven't taken down my old Geocities homepage, but it no longer exists.

36 Galloway, *Protocol*, 2.

37 Maeve Duggan and Aaron Smith, "Social Media Update 2013," *Pew Internet and American Life Project*, December 2013, accessed 18 July 2017, http://www.pewinternet.org/2013/12/30/social-media-update-2013/.

38 See, for example, Kevan Lee, "Decoding the Facebook News Feed: An Up-to-Date List of the Algorithm Factors and Changes," *BufferSocial*, 11 April 2014, accessed 18 July 2017, https://blog.bufferapp.com/facebook-news-feed-algorithm.

39 José van Dijck, *The Culture of Connectivity: A Critical History of Social Media* (Oxford: Oxford University Press, 2013), 41–2; emphasis in original.

40 Charles Sendlor, "Fan Fiction Statistics," *FFN Research* (blog), 18 March 2011, accessed 18 July 2017, http://ffnresearch.blogspot.com/2011/03/fan-fiction-demographics-in-2010-age.html.

41 On "Internet fame," see, for example, Joe Coscarelli, "The Weird Wide World of Internet Celebrity," *New York Magazine*, 20 April 2014, accessed 18 July 2017, http://nymag.com/news/features/internet-fame/; and Tad Friend, "Hollywood and Vine," *New Yorker*, 15 December 2014, accessed 18 July 2017, http://www.newyorker.com/magazine/2014/12/15/hollywood-vine.

42 Ethan Zuckerman, "The Cute Cat Theory Talk at ETech," *Ethan Zuckerman* (blog), 8 March 2008, accessed 18 July 2017, http://www.ethanzuckerman.com/blog/2008/03/08/the-cute-cat-theory-talk-at-etech/. The statement is the basis of the so-called "cute cat theory of media activism."

43 Possibly the most famous version of a "meme" being overlaid onto a different media item, and from there being developed into a new meme, is the Tumblr "Texts from Hillary," which borrowed its rubric from a meme called "Texts from Ryan Gosling." See Phoebe Connelly, "Texts from Hillary: Your New Favorite Political Tumblr," *Yahoo News*, 5 April 2012, accessed 18 July 2017, https://www.yahoo.com

/news/blogs/ticket/texts-hillary-favorite-political-tumblr-192421567.html.

44 Limor Shifman, *Memes in Digital Culture* (Cambridge, MA: MIT Press, 2014).

45 "This takes different forms in different games, but we can outline two basic ways in which games are structured and provide challenges for players: that of emergence (a number of simple rules combining to form interesting variations) and that of progression (separate challenges presented serially)." Jesper Juul, *Half-Real: Video Games Between Real Games and Fictional Worlds* (Cambridge, MA: MIT Press, 2005), 5. I discuss emergence further in chapter 3.

46 Van Dijck, *The Culture of Connectivity*; Lessig, *Code*; Galloway, *Protocol*. Of course, users can overcome some of those "rules" through creative subversion or technological intervention, thus changing the terms of play. For example, Kate Raynes-Goldie discusses, in the context of Facebook, "the somewhat subversive practices which users engag[e] in to enhance their own social privacy, and in some cases, violate that of others." Kate Raynes-Goldie, "Aliases, Creeping, and Wall Cleaning: Understanding Privacy in the Age of Facebook," *First Monday* 15, no. 1 (4 January 2010), accessed 18 July 2017, http://journals.uic.edu/ojs/index.php/fm/article/view/2775/2432. The metaphorical description of websites in terms of a front and back end appears in Richard Rogers, *Information Politics on the Web* (Cambridge, MA: MIT Press, 2004).

47 Antonio Ceraso, "Review; Postscript on Contribution Societies," *Criticism* 53, no. 3 (Summer 2011): 500. The term "prosumer" originated in 1980, when Alvin Toffler used it in his book *The Third Wave* as a way of describing the joining of producers and consumers into a single economic entity. Alvin Toffler, *The Third Wave* (New York: HarperCollins 1980), 282–305. For Toffler, the portmanteau "prosumer" joins the words "producer" and "consumer"; others have used the term to join "professional" and "consumer" or "proactive" and "consumer." The general meaning does not change.

48 Richard Barbrook, "The Hi-tech Gift Economy," *First Monday*, 5 December 2005, accessed 18 July 2017, http://journals.uic.edu/ojs/index.php/fm/article/view/631.

49 Clay Shirky, *Cognitive Surplus: Creativity and Generosity in a Connected Age* (New York: Penguin Press, 2010), 4–5.

50 Ibid., 86.

51 Ceraso, "Review; Postscript," 504.

52 Van Dijck, *The Culture of Connectivity*, 37.

53 Natasha Singer, "Can't Put Down Your Device? That's by Design," *New York Times*, 5 December 2015, accessed 18 July 2017, https://www.nytimes.com/2015/12/06/technology/personaltech/cant-put-down-your-device-thats-by-design.html.

54 The platform has sometimes courted controversy as a result, as when drag performers had to fight to be allowed to create profiles under their drag identities. Valeriya Safronova, "Drag Performers Fight Facebook's 'Real Name' Policy," *New York Times*, 24 September 2004, accessed 18 July 2017, https://www.nytimes.com/2014/09/25/fashion/drag-performers-fight-facebooks-real-name-policy.html.

55 As an aside, we may be able to gain some insight into social-media gaffes by regarding them in the context of the game mechanics on these platforms. Jon Ronson has been the most entertaining chronicler of the era of the social-media gaffe. As he emphasizes in his 2015 book on the subject, the fields of social media are littered with the metaphorical bodies of users who shared texts or pictures on social media that, to their entire surprise, brought about negative consequences in their "real lives." How can people not make the connection between their activity on the Internet and their lives outside of the Internet? One possible answer is that some users register the game mechanics on sites like Facebook and Twitter as a cue to treat their activity on these sites as they would treat any other game – that is, as circumscribed by a magic circle that protects their activity from consequence. But any magic circle is a broken circle at best; if I deliberately break another player's ankle in a soccer game, I incur consequences in real life. The game mechanics on these sites may engender a false lack of wariness. Jon Ronson, *So You've Been Publicly Shamed* (New York: Penguin Publishing Group, 2015).

56 Alvin Kernan, *Samuel Johnson and the Impact of Print* (1987; repr., Princeton: Princeton University Press, 1989), 8.

57 The character does not actually say this line in the film (*Wall Street*, 1987); however, previews for the film showed the character saying the line, and it quickly became famous.

## Chapter Three

1　Charles Sendlor, "Fan Fiction Statistics," *ffn Research* (blog), 18 March 2011, accessed 18 July 2017, http://ffnresearch.blogspot.com/2011/03 /fan-fiction-demographics-in-2010-age.html. Accounts of fan fiction as a predominantly female enterprise include Henry Jenkins, *Textual Poachers: Television Fans and Participatory Culture* (New York: Routledge, 1992); and Camille Bacon-Smith, *Enterprising Women: Television Fandom and the Creation of Popular Myth* (Philadelphia: University of Pennsylvania Press, 1992).

2　Sendlor, "Fan Fiction Statistics."

3　"Site Overview: Fanfiction.net," Alexa.com, accessed 8 January 2015, http://www.alexa.com/siteinfo/fanfiction.net.

4　See, for example, Bacon-Smith, *Enterprising Women*; Jenkins, *Textual Poachers*; Henry Jenkins and John Tulloch, eds, *Science Fiction Audiences: Watching Dr Who and Star Trek* (New York: Routledge, 1995); Matthew Hills, *Fan Cultures* (New York: Routledge, 2002); Henry Jenkins, *Fans, Bloggers, and Gamers: Exploring Participatory Culture* (New York: New York University Press, 2006); and Karen Hellekson and Kristina Busse, eds, *Fan Fiction and Fan Communities in the Age of the Internet: New Essays* (Jefferson, NC: McFarland & Company, 2006).

5　Steven A. Hetcher, "Using Social Norms to Regulate Fan Fiction and Remix Culture," *University of Pennsylvania Law Review* 157 (2009): 1870. Cited in Lawrence Lessig, *Remix: Making Art and Culture Thrive in the Hybrid Economy* (New York: The Penguin Press, 2008).

6　See, for example, Karen Hellekson, "A Fannish Field of Value: Online Fan Gift Culture," *Cinema Journal* 48, no. 4 (Summer 2009): 113–18.

7　See, for example, Jenkins, *Fans, Bloggers, and Gamers*; Jenkins, *Textual Poachers*; and Bacon-Smith, *Enterprising Women*.

8　See, for example, John Perry Barlow, "A Declaration of the Independence of Cyberspace," *Electronic Frontier Foundation* (8 February 1996), accessed 18 July 2017, https://www.eff.org/cyberspace-independence.

9　Lessig, *Remix*, 2–3.

10　See, for example, Lawrence Lessig, *Code: And Other Laws of Cyberspace, Version 2.0* (New York: Basic Books, 2006); and Jonathan

Zittrain, *The Future of the Internet – And How to Stop It* (New Haven, CT: Yale University Press, 2009).

11 Lessig, *Remix*. See also Charles Leadbeater and Paul Miller, *The Pro-Am Revolution: How Enthusiasts Are Changing Our Economy and Society* (London: Demos, 2004); Yochai Benkler, *The Wealth of Networks: How Social Production Transforms Markets and Freedom* (New Haven, CT: Yale University Press, 2007); and Clay Shirky, *Here Comes Everybody: The Power of Organizing without Organizations* (New York: Penguin, 2008).

12 As Steven Hetcher notes, "Lessig fails to identify Facebook as one of his hybrids that combines the amateur and the commercial." Steven Hetcher, "Amateur Creative Digital Content and Proportional Commerce," in *Amateur Media: Social, Cultural, and Legal Perspectives*, ed. Dan Hunter (New York: Routledge, 2013), 48ffn.

13 I treat these sites as social-media platforms because they are designed to facilitate social interaction among users and the circulation of user-generated content.

14 The origin of the concept of an imagined community is Benedict Anderson, *Imagined Communities: Reflections on the Origin and Spread of Nationalism* (London: Verso, 1983).

15 It may be significant that the installments of a serial are almost always separated by gaps – weekly gaps between television episodes, multi-year gaps between installments of a book series – which provide audience members with a necessary space within which to communicate, build elaborate social architectures, and create stories of their own. Where fan culture is concerned, the most important part of a serial is not the installments themselves, but rather the gaps between them.

16 On this history, see, for example, Nancy Fraser, "Rethinking the Public Sphere: A Contribution to the Critique of Actually Existing Democracy," in *Habermas and the Public Sphere*, ed. Craig Calhoun (Cambridge, MA: MIT Press, 1989): 109–42; and Michael Warner, *Publics and Counterpublics* (New York: Zone Books, 2002).

17 "AO3 Census: About You," *CentrumLumina* (blog), 2 October 2013, accessed 18 July 2017, http://centrumlumina.tumblr.com/post /62895609672/ao3-census-about-you. Demographically, users of social media, of which AO3 is a specialized subcategory, tend to be

teenagers and young adults. Some platforms, such as Pinterest and
Facebook, have slightly higher proportions of female users, while
others, such as Twitter, have slightly higher proportions of male
users; the dramatic gender imbalance on AO3 is unusual for social-
media platforms writ large, although it is typical for fan fiction platforms. The decision, on the part of AO3, to publish a census that
takes into account issues of gender and sexuality in such a fine grain
is likewise unusual for social-media sites but not unusual for a fan
site. See Shannon Greenwood, Andrew Perrin, and Maeve Duggan,
"The Demographics of Social Media Users in 2016," *Pew Research
Center*, 11 November 2016, accessed 18 July 2017, http://www.pew
internet.org/2016/11/11/social-media-update-2016/.

18  Ibid.

19  Home page, Archive of Our Own, 17 July 2018, accessed 10 July
2018, https://archiveofourown.org/.

20  Lessig, *Code*.

21  The blogger "obsession_inc" coined these terms in a now-famous
2009 blog post. Obsession_inc, "Affirmational Fandom vs. Transformational Fandom," *obsession-inc* (blog), 1 June 2009, accessed 18 July
2017, http://obsession-inc.dreamwidth.org/82589.html.

22  Archive of Our Own. Accessed 18 July 2017.

23  Roberta Pearson, "Bachies, Bardies, Trekkies, and Sherlockians," in
*Fandom: Identities and Communities in a Mediated World*, ed. Jonathan
Gray, Cornel Sandvoss, C. Lee Harrington (New York: New York
University Press, 2007), 98–109.

24  See, for example, Henry Jenkins, "On Mad Men, Aca-Fandom, and
the Goals of Cultural Criticism," *Confessions of an Aca-Fan: The Official Weblog of Henry Jenkins*, 11 August 2010, accessed 18 July 2017,
http://henryjenkins.org/blog/2010/08/on_mad_men_aca-fan_and
_the_nat.html.

25  Jerome McGann, "Database, Interface, and Archival Fever," *PMLA* 122,
no. 5 (October 2007): 1588.

26  Lessig, *Code*; Alexander Galloway, *Protocol: How Control Exists after
Decentralization* (Cambridge, MA: MIT Press, 2004); Jonathan Zittrain,
*The Future of The Internet – And How to Stop It* (New Haven, CT: Yale
University Press, 2008); William Mitchell, *City of Bits: Space, Place,
and the Infobahn* (Cambridge, MA: MIT Press, 1995), 111. See also Joel

Reidenberg, "Lex Informatica: The Formulation of Information Policy Rules through Technology," *Texas Law Review* 76 (1998): 553. Both are cited in Lessig, *Code*, 4.

27 Abigail Chen, "Harry Potter and the Raging Writers: When Fans Take Things to the Next Level," *College Hill Independent* (6 March, 2008), accessed 18 July 2017, http://www.theindy.org/a/1480.

28 See, for example, Richard Siklos, "A Virtual World but Real Money," *New York Times*, 19 October 2006, accessed 18 July 2017, http://www.nytimes.com/2006/10/19/technology/19virtual.html. Lessig also discusses Second Life in *Code*.

29 On identity and social media, see, for example, dana boyd, *It's Complicated: The Social Lives of Networked Teens* (New Haven, CT: Yale University Press, 2014).

30 For two classic discussions of the implications of this passage for our thinking about classification, see Michel Foucault, *The Order of Things: An Archeology of the Human Sciences* (New York: Vintage Books, 1973); and Robert Darnton, "Philosophers Trim the Tree of Knowledge," in *The Great Cat Massacre: And Other Episodes in French Cultural History* (Cambridge, MA: Harvard University Press, 1984), 191–214.

31 See, for example, the essays collected in "Remapping Genre," special issue, *PMLA* 122, no. 5 (October 2007).

32 The four classical types of narrative genre are romance, in which the protagonist struggles against the constraints of the world and ultimately transcends them; tragedy, in which the protagonist struggles against the constraints of the world and ultimately loses; comedy, in which the world of constraint and the world of the spirit are ultimately shown to be in harmony; and satire, which emphasizes the impossibility of making sense of the world using a structuring narrative. See, for example, Hayden White, *Metahistory: The Historical Imagination in Nineteenth-Century Europe* (Baltimore, MD: Johns Hopkins University Press, 1973).

33 Of course, the user could memorize some extremely specific tag string and use it to find that specific story. However, it would be far more practical to just remember the story's title or author.

34 "Terms of Service FAQ," Archive of Our Own. Accessed 11 July 2016.

35 And other communities like it; story exchange events of this kind

also take place on Tumblr and Fanfiction.net. Some websites revolve entirely around games of request and response, with the quality and number of stories posted measuring the success of a prompt and the number of comments posted measuring the success of a fill.

36 See, for example, Hellekson and Busse, *Fan Fiction and Fan Communities*, 10–11.

37 "What Is a 'Canonical' Tag?," Archive of Our Own. Accessed 18 July 2017, http://archiveofourown.org/faq/tags?language_id=en#what canonical.

38 Suki Kim writes about her experience, as an author, of seeing her publisher brand her book as a memoir in order to expand its readership, which she considers to be a misclassification. Suki Kim, "The Reluctant Memoirist," *New Republic*, 27 June 2016, accessed 18 July 2017, https://newrepublic.com/article/133893/reluctant-memoirist.

39 Ted Underwood, "Distant Reading and the Blurry Edges of Genre," *The Stone and the Shell* (blog), 22 October 2014, accessed 5 August 2016, https://tedunderwood.com/2014/10/22/distant-reading-and-the-blurry-edges-of-genre/.

40 Estimates of the word count of any literary work will, of course, vary; differences among translations and editions make definitive numbers virtually impossible to arrive at. These numbers are intended only as general estimates. Blue, "Great Novels and Word Count," *indefeasible* (blog), 3 May 2008, accessed 5 August 2016, https://indefeasible.wordpress.com/2008/05/03/great-novels-and-word-count/.

41 Colleen Lindsay, "All New & Revised: On Word Counts and Novel Length," *The Swivet* (blog), 19 September 2010, accessed 1 August 2016, http://theswivet.blogspot.com/2008/03/on-word-counts-and-novel-length.html.

42 AO3; search conducted on 18 July 2017.

43 Jane Smiley, *Thirteen Ways of Looking at the Novel* (New York: Alfred A. Knopf, 2005), 15.

44 AO3; search conducted on 18 July 2017.

45 Of course, as Lessig notes in another context, the potential audience for a digital work can far exceed the potential audience for a novel. Lessig, *Code*.

46 On this subject, see, especially, Jenkins, *Fans, Bloggers, and Gamers*; Jenkins, *Textual Poachers*; and Bacon-Smith, *Enterprising Women*.

47 Jenkins, *Fans, Bloggers, and Gamers*, 25.

48 Abigail Derecho, "A Definition, A History, and Several Theories of Fanfiction," in *Fan Fiction and Fan Communities in the Age of the Internet*, ed. Karen Hellekson and Kristina Busse (Jefferson, NC: McFarland and Company, 2006), 62. See also Jenkins, *Textual Poachers*.

49 See, for example, James English, *The Economy of Prestige: Prizes, Awards, and the Circulation of Cultural Value* (Cambridge, MA: Harvard University Press, 2005), 53.

50 Hellekson, "A Fannish Field of Value."

51 Alvin Kernan, *Samuel Johnson and the Impact of Print* (1987; repr., Princeton: Princeton University Press, 1989).

52 Marshall McLuhan and Benedict Anderson draw a direct connection between the technology of the printed book and the capitalist economy. Anderson, *Imagined Communities*, 33–4; Marshall McLuhan, *The Gutenberg Galaxy: The Making of Typographic Man* (Toronto: University of Toronto Press, 1962), 25.

53 Kathleen Fitzpatrick, *Planned Obsolescence: Publishing, Technology, and the Future of the Academy* (New York: New York University Press, 2011).

54 Alexander Galloway, *Gaming: Essays on Algorithmic Culture* (Minneapolis: University of Minnesota Press, 2006), 2.

55 Hellekson, "A Fannish Field of Value," 114.

56 Jesper Juul, *Half-Real: Video Games Between Real Games and Fictional Worlds* (Cambridge, MA: MIT Press, 2005), 12–13, emphasis added. Borges, meanwhile, maintained that rules in literature are necessary in order to perform the most exciting of literary moves, the turning of a corner into the unexpected: "Literature is a game with tacit conventions; to violate them partially or totally is one of the many joys (one of the many obligations) of the game, whose limits are unknown." Astrid Ensslin, *Literary Gaming* (Cambridge, MA: MIT Press, 2014), 28–9. But of course he was not describing a real game according to the minimal definition this essay uses.

57 Hellekson, "A Fannish Field of Value," 116.

58 For an account of "The Great Game" that traces the practice, if not the name, to 1902, see Zach Dundas, *The Great Detective: The Amaz-*

*ing Rise and Immortal Life of Sherlock Holmes* (New York: Houghton Mifflin Harcourt, 2015).

59 "Durable, if not permanent" because a story can continue to receive new points in perpetuity, enabling relative scores to change over time. However, a user can only award a point to a given story once, and a user cannot rescind a point that she has given.

60 Jenkins, *Textual Poachers*.

61 See, for example, Zach Waggoner, *My Avatar, My Self: Identity in Video Role-Playing Games* (Jefferson, NC: McFarland & Company, 2009); and Tom Boellstorff, Bonnie Nardi, Celia Pearce, and T.L. Taylor, *Ethnography and Virtual Worlds: A Handbook of Method* (Princeton: Princeton University Press, 2012), especially 60–140. Jesper Juul also discusses the relationship between players and avatars (*Half-Real*).

62 The administrators of AO3 might prefer to say that pseudonymity allows users to try new things, but the practical consequences are the same.

63 Brian Sutton-Smith argues that in the act of play, we interrogate not only the meaning of the activities we play at, but also the meaning of our identities as actors: "ludic performances are arranged to persuade ourselves (and others) to adopt the communal view of ourselves that we prefer ... metaphoric representations of our own identity in grand terms." Brian Sutton-Smith, *The Ambiguity of Play* (Cambridge, MA: Harvard University Press, 2001), 92.

64 Again, the measurement of the result using points, combined with the rules that the constraints set and the voluntariness of the activity, sets the activity categorically in the realm of game play.

## Chapter Four

1 Jonathan Sawday and Neil Rhodes, eds, *The Renaissance Computer: Knowledge Technology in the First Age of Print* (New York: Routledge, 2000).

2 Andreas S. Jucker, "Mass Media Communication at the Beginning of the Twenty-First Century: Dimensions of Change," *Journal of Historical Pragmatics* 4, no. 1 (2003): 129.

3  Sawaday and Rhodes, eds, *The Renaissance Computer*; Tom Standage, *The Victorian Internet: The Remarkable Story of the Telegraph and the Nineteenth Century's On-Line Pioneers* (New York: Bloomsbury, 1998); Tom Standage, *Writing on the Wall: Social Media – The First 2,000 Years* (New York: Bloomsbury, 2013); Leah Price, "Books as Social Media" (lecture, New York University, April 2014); Robert Darnton, "Blogging Now and Then (250 Years Ago)" (lecture, Harvard University, December 2012); John Brewer, "What's in a Visitor's Book? Social Media and Volcanic Tourism in the Nineteenth Century" (lecture, Harvard University, September 2013).

4  Alvin Kernan, *Samuel Johnson and the Impact of Print* (1987; repr., Princeton: Princeton University Press, 1989), 54.

5  See, for example, Thomas Pettit, "The Gutenberg Parenthesis: Oral Tradition and Digital Technologies" (lecture, Massachusetts Institute of Technology, April 2010). Video available at "Video and podcast: Thomas Pettit, 'The Gutenberg Parenthesis: Oral Tradition and Digital Technologies,'" *Comparative Media Studies and Writing* (blog), 14 April 2010, accessed 18 July 2017.

6  Jose-Antonio Cordon-Garcia, Julio Alonso-Arevalo, Raquel Gomez-Diaz, and Daniel Linder, "Towards a New Conception of Books and Reading," in *Social Reading: Platforms, Applications, Clouds, and Tags*, ed. (Oxford: Chandos Publishing, 2013), 25–43.

7  Walter J. Ong, *Orality and Literacy* (1982; repr., New York: Routledge, 2005), 207.

8  See, for example, Peter Stallybrass, "Against Thinking," *PMLA* 122 (2007): 1580–7.

9  Pettit, "Before the Gutenberg Parenthesis," 2.

10  Louise George Clubb, "Looking Back on Shakespeare and Italian Theater," in "Italy in the Drama of Europe," eds Albert Russell Ascoli and William I. West, special issue, *Renaissance Drama* 36, no. 37 (2010): 17.

11  Jill Walker Rettberg, "Blogs, Literacies, and the Collapse of Private and Public," *Leonardo Electronic Archive*, 16, nos 2–3 (2007): 8.

12  Thomas Pettit, "The Privacy Parenthesis: Gutenberg, *Homo Clausus*, and the Networked Self," lecture, April 2013.

13  Ibid.

14 Raymond Williams, *Television: Technology and Cultural Form* (1975; repr., New York: Schocken Books, 1977), 28.

15 Adrian Johns, *The Nature of the Book: Print and Knowledge in the Making* (Chicago: University of Chicago Press, 2009).

16 Michael Warner, *The Letters of the Republic: Publication and the Public Sphere in Eighteenth-Century America* (Cambridge, MA: Harvard University Press, 1990).

17 Leo Marx, "Technology: The Emergence of a Hazardous Concept," *Social Research* 64, no. 3 (Fall 1997): 965–88.

18 Ibid., 966–7.

19 *Oxford English Dictionary*, s.v. "Technology," accessed 7 December 2015.

20 Marx, "Technology," 967.

21 Ibid., 973.

22 Ibid., 978.

23 Ibid., 980.

24 Leo Marx, *The Machine in the Garden: Technology and the Pastoral Ideal in America* (1964; repr., Oxford: Oxford University Press, 2000), 187ffn.

25 Paul Duguid, "Getting Information from Books: A View of the 18th Century" (lecture, Harvard University, 4 February 2014).

26 Alan Hyde, *Working in Silicon Valley: Economic and Legal Analysis of a High-Velocity Labor Market* (New York: M.E. Sharpe, 2003), 7–10. On start-up culture, see also AnnaLee Saxenian, *Regional Advantage: Culture and Competition in Silicon Valley and Route 128* (Cambridge, MA: Harvard University Press, 1994); Chong Moon Lee, William F. Miller, Marguerite Gong Hancock, and Henry S. Rowen, eds, *The Silicon Valley Edge: A Habitat for Innovation and Entrepreneurship* (Stanford, CA: Stanford University Press, 2000); Douglas K. Smith and Robert C. Alexander, *Fumbling the Future: How Xerox Invented, Then Ignored, the First Personal Computer* (New York: Morrow, 1988); and Michael Hiltzik, *Dealers of Lightning: Xerox PARC and the Dawn of the Computer Age* (New York: Harper Business, 1999).

27 Clayton Christensen, *The Innovator's Dilemma: When New Technologies Cause Great Firms to Fail* (Cambridge, MA: Harvard Business Review Press, 1997).

28  Larissa McFarquhar, "When Giants Fail: What Business Has Learned from Clayton Christensen," *New Yorker*, 14 May 2012, 84–90.

29  Nicholas Carr, "IT Doesn't Matter," *Harvard Business Review* (May 2003), accessed 18 July 2017, https://hbr.org/2003/05/it-doesnt-matter.

30  Ibid.

31  Paul Levinson, *The Soft Edge: A Natural History and Future of the Information Revolution* (New York: Routledge, 1997); Charlene Li and Josh Bernhoff, *Groundswell: Winning in a World Transformed by Social Technologies* (Cambridge, MA: Harvard Business Review Press, 2011); Stuart Armstrong, *Smarter Than Us: The Rise of Machine Intelligence* (Berkeley, CA: Machine Intelligence Research Institute, 2014).

32  Christine Borgman, *From Gutenberg to the Global Information Infrastructure* (Cambridge, MA: MIT Press, 2000); Peter Shillingsburg, *From Gutenberg to Google: Electronic Representations of Literary Texts* (Cambridge: Cambridge University Press, 2006); John Naughton, *From Gutenberg to Zuckerberg: Disruptive Innovation in the Age of the Internet* (New York: Quercus, 2011).

33  Asa Briggs and Peter Burke, *Social History of the Media: From Gutenberg to the Internet* (Cambridge, UK: Polity, 2010), 5.

34  Nicholas Carr, *The Shallows: What the Internet Is Doing to Our Brains* (New York: W.W. Norton & Company, 2010), 10.

35  Bill Pascoe to Humanist Mailing List, 27 May 2016, accessed 18 July 2017.

36  See, for example, Michael Sean Mahoney, *Histories of Computing* (Cambridge, MA: Harvard University Press, 2011).

37  Pierre Bourdieu, "Flaubert and the French Literary Field," in *The Field of Cultural Production: Essays on Art and Literature*, trans. Randal Johnson (New York: Columbia University Press, 1993), 145–211.

38  Ibid., 172.

39  Ibid., 37–8.

40  José van Dijck, *The Culture of Connectivity: A Critical History of Social Media* (Oxford: Oxford University Press, 2013), 3.

41  Ibid., 21–2.

42  Lev Manovich, *The Language of New Media* (Cambridge, MA: MIT Press, 2001).

43  Ibid., 225.

44 N. Katherine Hayles, "Narrative and Database: Natural Symbionts," *PMLA* 122 (2007): 1603–8; N. Katherine Hayles, *How We Think: Digital Media and Contemporary Technogenesis* (Chicago: University of Chicago Press, 2012).

45 Lisa Gitelman, ed., *Raw Data Is an Oxymoron* (Cambridge, MA: MIT Press, 2013).

46 Jerome McGann, "Database, Interface, and Archival Fever," *PMLA* 122 (2007): 1588–92.

47 Ed Folsom, "Database as Genre: The Epic Transformation of Archives," *PMLA* 122 (2007): 1575–6. Alan Galey and Meredith McGill likewise suggest the limits of the discourse that contrasts narrative and database, although they do not focus on user interfaces. "The digital medium doesn't necessarily deliver us from the perceived rigidities of print"; instead, digital databases often reinforce the print conventions that they mean to liberate us from, for example by reiterating the canon of literary value. Alan Galey, "Signal to Noise: Designing a Digital Edition of The *Taming of a Shrew* (1594)," *College Literature* 36, no. 1 (2009): 40–65; Meredith McGill, "Remediating Whitman," *PMLA* 122 (2007): 1594.

48 Jay David Bolter, *Writing Space: The Computer, The Writer, and the History of Writing* (New York: L. Erlbaum Associates, 1991), 51.

49 Van Dijck, *The Culture of Connectivity*, 21.

50 Donald A. Norman, *The Design of Everyday Things* (1988; repr., New York: Basic Books, 2002).

51 Ibid., 17–25.

52 "Mental models … result from our tendency to form explanations of things. These models are essential in helping us understand experiences, predict the outcomes of our actions, and handle unexpected occurrences" (ibid., 38). If, with Jonathan Gottschall, we understand humans as "storytelling animals" – animals that have the production of narrative structures as an intrinsic part of their psychology and cognition – then any functional metaphor that humans use must have a narrative basis. Norman gives indications that he understands human psychology to work in this way; but such an understanding is not necessary in order to recognize that explanations and instructions, including the kind grounded by interface metaphors, are time-

based processes. Jonathan Gottschall, *The Storytelling Animal: How Stories Make Us Human* (Boston: Houghton Mifflin Harcourt, 2012).

53  Frank Kessler and Mirko Tobias Schaefer, "Navigating YouTube: Constituting a Hybrid Information Management System," in *The YouTube Reader*, ed. Pelle Snickars and Patrick Vondereau (Stockholm: National Library of Sweden, 2009), 275.

54  The film scholar Leo Enticknap has reinforced this difference: "I don't see any evidence that YouTube is attempting to undertake long-term preservation of any of the material it hosts, which is surely a core function of an archive; one which distinguishes an archive from other types of document or media collection." Quoted in Kessler and Schaefer, "Navigating YouTube," 276.

55  Ibid., 276–7.

56  See, for example, Elyse Graham, "When Facebook Came to Princeton," *Princeton Alumni Weekly*, 1 June 2016, accessed 1 June 2016, https://paw.princeton.edu/article/when-facebook-came-princeton.

57  See, for example, Shanyang Zhao, Sherri Grasmuck, and Jason Martin, "Identity Construction on Facebook: Digital Empowerment in Anchored Relationships," *Computers in Human Behavior* 24, no. 5 (2008): 1816–36.

58  "The media coverage and resultant discourse surrounding social networking sites such as Facebook, MySpace and Friendster contain narratives of inevitability and technological determinism that require careful explication." Ryan Bigge, "The Cost of (Anti-)Social Networks: Identity, Agency and Neo-Luddites," *First Monday* 11, no. 12 (4 December 2006), accessed 18 July 2017, http://firstmonday .org/article/view/1421/1339.

59  Steven E. Jones, *Against Technology: From the Luddites to Neo-Luddism* (New York: Routledge, 2006), 174–5; quoted in Bigge, "The Cost of (Anti-) Social Networks."

60  See, for example, dana boyd, *It's Complicated: The Social Lives of Networked Teens* (New Haven, CT: Yale University Press, 2014).

61  Bigge, "The Cost of (Anti-) Social Networks."

62  G. Lovink, "The Art of Watching Databases," in *The Video Vortex Reader: Responses to YouTube*, ed. G. Lovink and S. Niederer (Amsterdam: Institute of Network Cultures, 2008), 9.

63  Ibid.

64  Ibid., 9–10.

65  Manovich, *The Language of New Media*, 200. See also Jessica Press-
    man, *Digital Modernism: Making It New in New Media* (Oxford: Ox-
    ford University Press, 2014), especially ch. 4.

66  Kessler and Schaefer, "Navigating YouTube," 276.

67  See also the special issue of *AI & Society*, "Database Aesthetics: Issues
    of Organization and Category in Art," ed. Victoria Vesna and David
    Smith, 14, no. 2 (2000); and Alan Liu, *Local Transcendence: Essays on
    Postmodern Historicism and the Database* (Chicago: University of
    Chicago Press, 2008).

68  Kessler and Schaefer, "Navigating YouTube," 276.

69  Stuart Moulthrop, "From Work to Play: Molecular Structure in the
    Time of Deadly Games," in *First Person: Narrative as Story Performance,
    and Game*, ed. Noah Wardrip-Fruin and Pat Harrigan (Cambridge,
    MA: MIT Press, 2004), 60.

70  "It can hardly have escaped anyone that YouTube presents videos in
    conjunction with viewer statistics, not detailed user profiles. As a
    matter of fact, 'users' are by definition reducible to quantified traces
    of actual usage. With views, clicks, comments, and ratings counted,
    user behavior becomes a byproduct of all the informational transac-
    tions taking place on the site, and raw data constantly gets fed back
    into the YouTube machinery." Pelle Snickars and Patrick Vonderau,
    "Introduction," *The YouTube Reader*, 16.

71  Manovich, *The Language of New Media*, 225.

72  Janet H. Murray, "The Last Word on Ludology v Narratology" (lec-
    ture, Digital Games Research Association, Vancouver, Canada, 17
    June 2005). Reprinted in *Inventing the Medium* (blog), 28 June 2013,
    accessed 18 July 2017, https://inventingthemedium.com/2013/06/28
    /the-last-word-on-ludology-v-narratology-2005/.

73  Espen Aarseth, "Blog Entry on Umea Aarseth/Jenkins Debate"
    (2005); quoted in Murray, "The Last Word on Ludology." No longer
    accessible online.

74  Murray, "The Last Word on Ludology."

75  Espen Aarseth, "Genre Trouble: Narrativism and the Art of Simula-
    tion," in *First Person: New Media as Story, Performance, and Game*, ed.
    Pat Harrington and Noah Wardrip-Fruin (Cambridge, MA: MIT Press,
    2004): 45–7.

76 "Instead of promoting power sharing, the contemporary deploy-
ment of interactivity exploits participation as a form of labor." An-
drejevic 2004.

## Chapter Five

1 Langdon Winner, "Do Artifacts Have Politics?," *Daedalus* 109, no. 1
(1980): 121–36.

2 For example, in a 2012 review of a new edition of the *Princeton Encyclopedia of Poetry and Poetics* (2012), Stephen Burt observes that many
of the entries differ considerably from the 1993 version of the same
work. Entries in the later version, he reported, include "more history,
more attention to a larger stack of ethnic and national traditions,
more discussion of how big terms (such as 'Romanticism') themselves have histories." On the whole, he says, the PEPP is moving
"away from prescriptive theory … towards a sense that almost everything about poetry (to quote Elizabeth Bishop) 'is historical, flow-
ing, and flown.'" Stephen Burt, "No More Rules," *London Review of
Books*, 19 November 2012, accessed 18 July 2017, https://www.lrb.co
.uk/blog/2012/11/19/stephen-burt/no-more-rules/.

3 Lawrence Lessig, *Remix: Making Art and Culture Thrive in the Hybrid
Economy* (New York: The Penguin Press, 2008). See also Axel Bruns,
who prefers the term "produsers": Axel Bruns, *Blogs, Wikipedia, Second Life, and Beyond: From Production to Produsage* (New York: Peter
Lang, 2008).

4 H.A. Mason, *Humanism and Poetry in the Early Tudor Period: An Essay*
(London: Routledge and Kegan Paul, 1959). His argument is based
on the observation that the history of courtly love poems is also a
history of the continual rearrangement of stock materials, such as set
phrases, literary elements like alliteration, and conventional postures
on the lover's part. "Can we doubt that if we had all the songs sung
at court between Chaucer and Wyatt we should be able to show that
every word and phrase used by Wyatt was a commonplace and had
been used by many of his predecessors?" He concludes that in much
of the poetry produced for the Tudor court there is "not the slightest
trace of poetic activity," since "Wyatt, like the other court writers, was
merely supplying material for social occasions." Ibid., 160–71.

5 Christian Fuchs, Kees Boersma, Anders Albrechtslund, and Marisol Sandoval, eds, *Internet and Surveillance: The Challenges of Web 2.0 and Social Media* (New York: Routledge, 2012). John Palfrey has discussed state surveillance of social media, when users are aware that it is taking place, as a censorship practice that can be more effective than explicit blocks or filters. John Palfrey, "Four Phases of Internet Regulation," *Social Research* 77, no. 3 (Fall 2010): 981–96.

6 Van Dijck comments that, on social-media platforms, "data generation has become a primary objective rather than a by-product of online sociality." José van Dijck, *The Culture of Connectivity: A Critical History of Social Media* (Oxford: Oxford University Press, 2013), 12.

7 Marshall McLuhan, *The Gutenberg Galaxy: The Making of Typographic Man* (Toronto: University of Toronto Press, 1962). Few scholars subscribe any longer to the most extreme version of the concept of "print logic," the view that a technology can possess an inherent logic with a teleological aim.

8 Adam Kirsch, "Technology Is Taking Over English Departments," *New Republic*, 2 May 2014, accessed 18 July 2017, https://newrepublic.com/article/117428/limits-digital-humanities-adam-kirsch.

9 Alvin Kernan, *Samuel Johnson and the Impact of Print* (1987; repr., Princeton: Princeton University Press, 1989).

10 Robert Darnton, "Writing News and Telling Stories," *Daedalus* 104 (1975): 175–94.

11 Ibid., 176–7.

12 "The White House Maker Faire: 'Today's DIY Is Tomorrow's "Made in America,"'" *White House Blog*, 18 June 2014, accessed 18 July 2017, https://obamawhitehouse.archives.gov/blog/2014/06/18/president-obama-white-house-maker-faire-today-s-diy-tomorrow-s-made-america.

13 "The Global Cardboard Challenge: Just Build It!," *Imagination Foundation* (blog), 27 September 2016, accessed 18 July 2017, http://educatorinnovator.org/the-global-cardboard-challenge-just-build-it/.

14 See, for example, Lev Manovich, *The Language of New Media* (Cambridge, MA: MIT Press, 2001); and Yochai Benkler, *The Wealth of Networks: How Social Production Transforms Markets and Freedom* (New Haven, CT: Yale University Press, 2006).

15 Robert McMillan, "The White House Gives Up on Making Coders Dress Like Adults," *Wired*, 21 August 2014, accessed 18 July 2017, https://www.wired.com/2014/08/the-white-house-dickerson/.

16 See, for example, Francesca Polletta and James M. Jasper, "Collective Identity and Social Movements," *Annual Review of Sociology* 27 (2001); and Debra Friedman and Doug McAdam, "Collective Identity and Activism: Networks Choices and the Life of a Social Movement," in *Frontiers in Social Movement Theory*, ed. Aldon D. Morris and Carol M. Mueller (New Haven: Yale University Press, 1992), 156–73. Along similar lines, in his 1975 essay, Darnton draws on a body of sociological research that investigates how we acquire the norms and occupational frameworks belonging to different fields. The theme of this field of research, which was especially popular during the 1970s, is sentimental education: not the textbooks that medical students memorize, but rather how medical students learn to think like doctors. Seminal early works in the sociology of occupations include John van Maanen, "Observations on the Making of Policemen," *Human Organization* 32: 407–17; Robert Merton, "Some Preliminaries to a Sociology of Medical Education," in *The Student-Physician: Introductory Studies in the Sociology of Medical Education*, ed. Robert Merton, George G. Reader, and Patricia L. Kendall (Cambridge, MA: Harvard University Press, 1957); and Everett C. Hughes, *Men and Their Work* (Westport, CT: Greenwood Press, 1958).

17 I have found the work of social-movement theorists like Jasper, cited in the note above, useful in understanding how people become members of the high-tech community. Sociologists sometimes use the term "identity work" to describe the deliberate efforts that members of social movements undertake in order to forge and sustain a collective identity. The members of a group may take up the group's symbols and mannerisms in order to assert their kinship, share an emotional bond, or sustain their reputations in one another's eyes. Indeed, maintaining a good reputation in one group may oblige you to participate in another: for example, being an activist with being a churchgoer, or being a programmer with being a gamer.

18 See, for example, Fred Turner, *From Counterculture to Cyberculture: Stewart Brand, The Whole Earth Network, and the Rise of Digital Utopianism* (Chicago: University of Chicago Press, 2006); Richard Bar-

brook and Andy Cameron, "The California Ideology," *Science as Culture* 26 (1996): 44–72; Langdon Winner, "Peter Pan in Cyberspace"; and Langdon Winner, "Techné and Politeia: The Technical Constitution of Society," in *Philosophy and Technology*, ed. Paul T. Durbin and Fredrich Rapp (Dordrecht: D. Reidel, 1983), 97–111.

19  Molly Sauter, *The Coming Swarm: DDOS Actions, Hacktivism, and Civil Disobedience on the Internet* (New York: Bloomsbury Academic, 2014).

20  Nelson D. Schwartz, "Facing WikiLeaks Threat, Bank Plays Defense," *New York Times*, 2 January 2011, accessed 18 July 2017, http://www .nytimes.com/2011/01/03/business/03wikileaks-bank.html.

21  Kathleen Fitzpatrick discusses, in this connection, bodies of scholarly editors; N. Katherine Hayles discusses authors of literary hypertexts; and Luis Murillo discusses computer hackers. See Kathleen Fitzpatrick, *Planned Obsolescence: Publishing, Technology, and the Future of the Academy* (New York: New York University Press, 2011); N. Katherine Hayles, *How We Think: Digital Media and Contemporary Technogenesis* (Chicago: University of Chicago Press, 2012); and Luis Felipe Murillo, "Transnationality, Morality, and Politics of Computing Expertise" (PhD diss., University of California, 2015).

22  C.P. Snow, *The Two Cultures* (1959; repr., Cambridge: Cambridge University Press, 1998).

23  Lev Manovich, *Software Takes Command* (New York: Bloomsbury Academic, 2013), 80.

24  A colleague who works in civic media recently posted a picture of his wedding vows to Facebook. One of his acquaintances expressed confusion in a comment post: "Are you two cosplaying?"

25  Jonathan Gottschall, *The Storytelling Animal: How Stories Make Us Human* (New York: Mariner Books, 2013).

26  Jonathan Gottschall, "Storytelling Animals: 10 Surprising Ways That Story Dominates Our Lives," *Huffington Post*, 21 April 2012, accessed 18 July 2017, http://www.huffingtonpost.com/jonathan-gottschall /humans-story-telling_b_1440917.html.

27  Brian Sutton-Smith, *The Ambiguity of Play* (Cambridge, MA: Harvard University Press, 2001), 3–5.

28  See, for example, Michael Sean Mahoney, *Histories of Computing* (Cambridge, MA: Harvard University Press, 2011); Jonathan Zittrain,

*The Future of the Internet and How to Stop It* (New Haven, CT: Yale University Press, 2008).

29  Discussions of the genealogies of new media still carry the burden of direct implications for university practice, even if the set of disciplines that participate in these discussions has widened. For example, if, following Lev Manovich, we see certain formal features of new media as evidence that new media has cinema as its closest antecedent, then we should embed film studies in the syllabus for new media studies. Whereas if the textual basis of most of our communication in new media, along with the inarguable claim that "books are machines," show that new media has the media of bibliographic production as its closest antecedent, then we can look to the history of books as our primary blueprint for the future of information. When McGann, writing in the 2010s, describes the book as a machine, or when George Landow, writing in the 1990s, describes hypertext as a book, they are contributing – in different decades, with different theoretical emphases, but in one common practical respect – to a strategic disciplinary tradition by which scholars of literature have sought to claim ownership of the digital medium by framing it as an extension of earlier, literary, formats.

# Index

Barthes, Roland, 120
Benkler, Yochai, 8, 114
Biblical hermeneutics, 64
blogging, 24–7, 31, 81
blogosphere, 16
Bogost, Ian, 30–2, 34, 50, 108,
    134n6. *See also* gamification;
    pointsification
bookmarks, 11, 58, 59, 61, 64, 73
books: end of, 85, 107; and games,
    5, 51, 79; and genre, 66; as
    metaphor, 4, 10, 96, 99–100,
    110, 158n29; the study of,
    17–18, 128n19, 146n52. *See also*
    e-books; literature; print
    culture
bookstores, 14, 110
Borges, Jorge Luis, 63, 73, 146n56
Bourdieu, Pierre, 18, 80, 97
"browsing," 15, 44, 52, 57, 102,
    127n7
bullshit, 31, 133n1
Buzzfeed, 45

Callois, Roger, 35–6, 39, 45
canon: fan fiction, 64–5, 66, 67,
    73; literary, 20, 151n47. *See also*
    "headcanons"; tagging
*Canterbury Tales* (Chaucer), 71
capitalism, 22, 23, 25, 97, 146n52.
    *See also* "ludic capitalism"
Carr, Nicolas, 93–4, 95–6
Carroll, Lewis, 73
Cerquiglini, Bernard, 13, 16–17
Chaucer, Geoffrey, 76, 154n4. See
    also *Canterbury Tales*

Christensen, Clayton, 93
Clemens, Samuel (Mark Twain),
    76
"cloud, the," 43
code, 15, 19; constraints of, 38, 54,
    60; modification of, 21; of so-
    cial media sites, 52, 62, 76, 78–9,
    103. *See also* digital platforms;
    "modding"
comments, 123n2; on Facebook,
    42, 48, 137n28; on fan fiction
    sites, 53, 59, 61, 63–4, 144n35; as
    scoring mechanism, 3, 6, 37–9,
    70; on YouTube, 103, 153n70.
    *See also* feedback; "likes";
    "shares"
communications, 9–10, 83, 92;
    digital, 49, 96, 117, 126n5;
    "mass," 87; studies, 81. *See also*
    media studies; new media; new
    media studies; oral culture;
    print culture
computer games, 21, 34–5, 40, 73,
    116, 135n12
"content farms," 26–8
copyright law, 53, 56. *See also*
    intellectual property
crowdsourcing, 27
"cyber-communism," 25
cyberculture, 131n42
cyberspace, 43, 53, 60

Darnton, Robert, 49, 81, 112–13,
    156n16
database: and interfaces, 58, 80–1,
    151n47; and marketing, 28; in

trade press, 12, 15, 85, 94. *See also* publishing

"trending," 6, 36, 38, 43–4, 124n6

Tumblr, 43, 52, 54, 77, 138n43, 144n35

Twain, Mark (Samuel Clemens), 76

Twitter, 5, 44, 124n6, 126n5, 142n17; activism on, 49; and free labour, 46; game mechanics of, 13, 41, 43, 45, 107, 140n55. *See also* hashtags; social media; "trending"

user interface. *See* interface

van Dijck, José, 5–6, 18, 43–4, 98, 100, 124n5, 126n5, 155n6

Veblen, Thorstein, 88

video games. *See* computer games

"viral" status, 6, 46, 83, 109

*Walt Whitman Archive*, 99

Web 2.0, 4–5, 28, 105, 123n2

WikiLeaks, 116

Williams, Raymond, 86–7, 89

Winner, Langdon, 106, 115

*Wired* magazine, 27, 111, 114–15

Wittgenstein, Ludwig, 35

Woolf, Virginia, 55

work. *See* labour

writers, 20, 40, 48; as content producers, 27–9, 53, 67; profiles of, 52, 54, 74. *See also* amateur fiction; author; fan fiction; labour; prosumers

YouTube: as an archive, 100–1, 152n54; content on, 8, 29, 153n70; game mechanics of, 13, 43; as part of an ecosystem, 5, 102–4; as social-media site, 45, 124n5. *See also* comments; database; social media

Zimmerman, Eric, 35

"zines," 74

Zuckerberg, Mark, 4, 82, 95